Becoming Financially Secure

What You Need To Know

By: Golden Noir-Fatale

Certified Financial Planner and Certified Public Accountant

Thanks!

ISBN-13: 978-1-4927-1649-5

ISBN-10:   1-4927-1649-9

To my clients who let me serve them for many decades. To all my teachers and students who have both taught me so much. To my friends and family that have always been there for me. Finally, to my wife, for everything, including the impossible task of trying to clean up my atrocious grammar in this book.

Table of Contents

AUTHOR'S NOTE

Thank you for taking the time to read this. For many decades I sat in an office with impressive framed pieces of paper on my wall and tried to be clever and wise for my clients in my practice. Also, as a hobby, I started teaching classes about finances and taxes at the graduate and undergraduate level at some local universities. In recent years, I have taught MBA students about personal financial planning. I have always been struck by how much even MBA students could benefit from a basic understanding of personal finances.

Now, it is time to leave my office, my practice and my clients and do other things with my life. I believe I have found a good home for my clients, but I will no longer be there in person to answer questions and provide guidance.

I wanted to leave my clients with a book that had some basic good educational material about achieving financial security. However, to my frustration, I could not find that book. For years, I have looked for a book, any book, that explained the basics of how to achieve financial security. To my mind, it is just not that complicated.

Most books on the topic are harmless enough, most of the time. However, they tend to bore you with useless information, and leave out vital things. Also, occasionally, some books will recommend you do something dangerous or stupid. In the end, I reluctantly decided the only solution was to write a book myself.

So, here it is. This book will try to explain the basic principles of how you can achieve financial security. As I said before, the basic principles of financial security are just not that complicated, but many of us never got good information on what we should do and routinely make mistakes that can hurt our financial security. For example, the real average person making real average investments does a terrible job of it. It is simple and easy to do much better once you know what you should do.

I suggest you just jump to whatever part of this book has the most interest for you. You may want to eventually look at the entire book to make sure you get a complete picture.

This book is intended for educational purposes only. It is not intended to be investment or tax advice. Also, as I like to keep a low profile, the name of the author on this book is a mashup of my pets' names rather than my actual name.

Finally, I want to apologize for writing such a long book. I did not have the time to write a shorter book. I wish you the best of luck in achieving financial security and reaching your goals and dreams.

PLANNING TO BECOME FINANCIALLY SECURE

Why You Need To Plan

If you want to become financially secure, you can rely on good luck, you can rely on divine intervention, or you can rely on planning. Personally, I recommend that you rely on planning. Becoming financially secure through planning is a realistic strategy. Becoming financially secure through good luck or divine intervention is a hope, not a plan.

The best time for you to start planning is right now. Waiting too long to plan is one of the big mistakes many people make. The sooner you start planning, the easier it will be for you.

How To Plan

Planning to become financially secure, or any type of planning for that matter, has five basic steps. These steps are

Where do you want to end up?

Where are you now?

How do you get from where you are now to where you want to end up?

Actually getting from where you are now to where you want to end up

Periodically updating your planning

Where Do You Want To End Up?

We all are going to end up somewhere whether we plan or not. You may as well end up closer to where you actually want to end up. If you have a clear idea of where you would like to end up, then the chance that you will end up there increases dramatically.

So, where do you want to end up? What is important to you? What is unimportant to you? What would you like to have and do in your life? What don't you care if you have and do in your life? Some people don't know the answers to these questions. Some people do.

What if you don't know where you want to end up? Some people just have a difficult time deciding what they like and where they would like to end up. If this is you, ask yourself where you do NOT want to end up. Think of the worst places that you could possibly end up. Once you decide on the worst places, ask yourself why these are the worst places for you to end up. What do you really hate about these worst places? Once have explored that, ask yourself where can I end up that is the opposite of these worst places? This will be a good start as to where you want to end up.

If you have a clear idea of where you want to end up, ask yourself why. What is it about your goal that makes it attractive to you? I would highly recommend that you understand not only your goal, but why you want to reach your goal. For example, let's say you want to end up with a net worth of $1 million. Why is that important to you? One person with that goal might want to feel financially secure and having a net worth of $1 million would accomplish that for the person. Another person with the same $1 million goal may be driven by the dream of gloating about their net worth to less financially successful friends or family members. Yet another person with the same goal $1 million goal may be seeking to devote his or her life to making the world a better place through charitable contributions. At first glance, you may think that each person in my example has the same goal. However, if you dig down a little bit, you discover that each person wants very different things.

Now, I know this is a book about achieving financial security, but finances can be a small part of most people's goals and dreams. Don't get me wrong. It is much better to be financially secure than not financially secure. However, most of us have goals and dreams other than just money. I recommend that you decide what your goals and dreams are first, and then figure out the finances you need to reach your goals and dreams.

Where Are You Now?

To decide where you are now, we use variations of two venerable financial statements, the balance sheet and the income statement. I apologize in advance to those of you with an accounting background for the way these two financial statements are presented in this book. One of the fancy pieces of paper on my wall is a certified public accountant license, and I do know better. However, given the points I'm trying to make, the presentation in this book makes the most sense to me.

The balance sheet has three parts. The first part is assets. Assets are good things like the cash in your wallet, the fair market value of your car or home, and the fair market value of your investments. The second part is debts or liabilities. Debts or liabilities are not so good things like the loan that you owe on your car or your home. If we add up the value of all of your assets, and we then subtract the value of all of your debts or liabilities, we end up with the third part of the balance sheet, your net worth.

The income statement also has three parts. The first part is income or increases in wealth like the paycheck from your work. The second part is expenses or decreases in wealth like the money you pay for groceries and rent. If we add up all of your income or increases in wealth, and then we subtract all of your expenses or decreases in wealth, we end up with the third part of the income statement, your change in net worth.

Now, let's say hypothetically, that you are choosing between two vacations to take, and you will make your decision based only on reaching your financial goal of becoming rich which you define as having a much higher net worth than you currently have. The first choice is a vacation that costs $50,000 flying around the world first class, staying at the most expensive hotels, visiting the most expensive tourist attractions. The second choice is a vacation that costs $500 camping in a tent in state parks in your state. Which vacation do you choose if you are making your decision based only on your goal of becoming rich by increasing your net worth?

Well, where does this vacation go on our two financial statements? The answer is that vacation, like most of your costs of living, is an expense or decrease in wealth on the income

5

statement. Holding everything else on your financial statements constant, what impact does each of these two vacations have on your net worth and your financial goal of becoming rich? The answer is that each vacation reduces your net worth. So, if you want to become rich, you should choose to go camping.

The reason I bring this up is that some people are confused about the difference between being rich and having a high cost of living. Some people believe that if they have high incomes and are spending lots and lots of money, they must be rich. People who spend lots and lots of money are not necessarily rich. You are rich if you have a high net worth. If you have a high income, spend it all, and have no net worth, you are not rich. You just have a high cost of living.

Having a high cost of living actually detracts from being rich. It is a definitional thing. If you want to become rich, over time you have to have more money coming into your life than is going out of your life. When this happens, your net worth goes up. When your net worth goes up to a certain point, you are rich.

How Do You Get From Where You Are Now To Where You Want To End Up?

That is basically where this book comes in. You can do most of it on your own. If you decide to hire people to help you, you want to hire competent and honest people. I personally believe in hiring the best people I can afford for everything from car mechanics to surgeons. I may not need the best, but, I would rather have the capability and not use it than need the capability and not have it. Ideally, you will be the typical customer for any person that you hire. That way, the person that you hire will have lots and lots of experience dealing with people just like you and is probably pretty good at it.

Actually Getting From Where You Are Now To Where You Want To End Up

Actually getting from where you are now to where you want to end up is the hardest part of any planning, including planning to become financially secure. It is sort of like losing weight. The hard part is not understanding what you need to do. The hard part is actually doing it.

Periodically Updating Your Planning

You do not just plan once. You change over time, and your goals and dreams will also change over time. As your goals and dreams change, you need to make sure that your planning is also changing. You want to periodically evaluate where you are now, where you want to be, and how you are going to get there.

PLANNING AND YOUR ATTITUDES TOWARDS RISK

There are many wonderful and useful mathematical tools and calculations that can be done to help you to achieve financial security. However, almost all of these calculations assume that you have a risk preference that may be very different from your actual risk preference.

Almost every mathematical tool or computation done as part of financial planning assumes that you have a neutral risk preference. A neutral risk preference generally means that within your body beats a calculating machine rather than a human heart. If you have a neutral risk preference, you will be happy doing whatever the numbers tell you to do. In my experience, people who have a neutral risk preference are rare.

Most of us do not have a neutral risk preference. Most of us have a risk-averse risk preference. What this means is that most of us do not like taking risks with things, including our finances, even if mathematically we would be financially better off if we took more risks. Most of us are just hardwired to be risk-averse and avoid taking even rational risks.

So, because most of us have a risk-averse risk preference, before you start using any simple or complicated mathematical tool or technique to guide your finances, you need to honestly assess what your personal risk preferences is. I would like to emphasize the word honestly.

If, for example, you know that you should really take a certain amount of risk with your retirement plan investments even if you are actually not comfortable with that risk, and you actually take more risk than you are comfortable with, bad things are inevitably going to happen to you in the future. What will most likely happen to you in my example is that sometime in the future the value of your retirement plan assets will inevitably go down so far you really will not be able to sleep at night. When this happens, you will likely end up selling your retirement plan investments. In other words, you will buy high and sell low. Not a good way to invest for retirement. This will not happen if you are honest with yourself about your actual risk preference from the beginning.

BUDGETING

In financial planning, budgeting is almost always recommended, and almost never done for long. It takes lots of financial discipline to follow a budget. But, if you have lots of financial discipline, you might not need a budget.

Here are some tips to actually increase the odds that you can follow a budget. First, put money into your budget for fun stuff. You should have a separate line item that says fun stuff. For many of us, following a budget is a grim, grim thing. Explicitly building in money for fun makes budgeting slightly less grim and gives you a higher chance of success. Second, put money into your budget for unanticipated things. What will they be? Who knows? You do not anticipate them. If you knew what they were, you would have a separate line item for them. Inevitably, something will come up that you did not anticipate when you made your budget. If you have money in your budget for unanticipated things, this is not as big of a problem.

Here is a very non-mainstream alternative to budgeting. If you are not already doing so, start keeping track of where you spend all of your money, and I mean all of your money. Put it into whatever categories make sense to you. How you view the world will drive what categories you use. For example, at one time the artist Vincent Van Gogh, who could really spend lots of money, decided in financial desperation to start tracking where he spent his money. In his world view, there were only 3 categories, art related expenses, ladies of the evening, and other. I would probably recommend more categories for you.

The immediate goal of tracking where you spend all of your money is to gather information, not change your behavior. At the end of some time, probably three months at a minimum, add up the totals of each of your categories. Then, look at the totals and ask yourself a simple question. Is this what I really want to spend my money on? More precisely, how much utility or happiness are you getting from each one of your expenditures?

Ideally, the end result of doing this is to reduce the amount of money that you are spending on the stuff you don't really get a lot of utility or happiness from, increase the amount of money that you are spending on stuff that you get lots of utility or happiness from, and reduce your overall expenses. In this ideal world you will end up spending less and getting more utility or happiness. Please note that this is the theory, and your actual results may vary.

WHAT IF YOU NEVER HAVE ANY MONEY LEFT TO SAVE?

If you earn a decent income but never seem to have any money left to save, consider paying yourself first. Paying yourself first is putting money into your savings first rather than if anything is left over after your expenses. A good way to pay yourself first and boost your savings is to have money taken out of your paycheck and automatically put into your savings or into your retirement plan. If it never ends up in your wallet, you can't spend it.

What if money is so tight right now that you cannot pay yourself first? If you are used to living off your current income, then you may consider putting part or all of any future income increases into savings. For example, if you get a salary increase or a bonus at work, consider putting part or all of that money into your savings before you get used to spending the new money.

FIRST THINGS FIRST, THE EMERGENCY RESERVE

If you want to become financially secure, one of the first things that you should do is get an emergency reserve. An emergency reserve is just a way to pay for the inevitable emergencies that come along in your life. Emergencies tend to crop up at unpredictable intervals. If you don't have a way to pay for the costs associated with an emergency, then any emergency can wipe you out financially. If you lose your job or your car's engine blows up, how are you going to pay the expenses of your life? This is where an emergency reserve comes in.

The traditional rule of thumb is that you need an emergency reserve in cash equal to six months of your salary. Like most traditional financial rules of thumb, it is better than nothing, but leaves room for improvement.

The origin of this traditional rule of thumb is as follows. For most of us, the biggest financial emergency would be paying for our costs of living if we lost our job. The traditional rule of thumb of six months of your salary assumes that the expenses of your life are approximately equal to your salary, and also assumes that it will take you approximately 6 months to find a new job. Therefore, you end up with a traditional rule of thumb that says you should have an emergency reserve in cash equal to six months of your salary.

Should you just use the traditional rule of thumb of six months of salary to calculate how much of an emergency reserve you need? Well, no. I would highly recommend you look at your particular situation rather than relying upon the traditional rule of thumb. For example, if you lost your job how would you pay for your costs of living until you found a new job? If you are in the fortunate position of having easy to transfer job skills that are in demand in a booming industry, it would probably take you less than six months to find a new job. On the other hand, if you have hard to transfer job skills in a depressed industry, it would probably take you more than six months to find a new job.

Once you have decided on the amount of your emergency reserve, do you really need to have this in cash in a bank account somewhere? Probably not. The goal of an emergency reserve is to have access to cash in an emergency. Actually having the cash set aside is fine, but you do have alternatives. Your alternatives include selling your investments, charging up your credit cards, drawing on a home equity line of credit, or perhaps borrowing from the National Bank of Friends and Family.

Remember, the idea behind an emergency reserve is for you to have access to enough cash in an emergency so you do not get wiped out financially. Setting up an emergency reserve is an early step for you to become financially secure.

CREDIT AND YOU

Credit Scoring

Most of us have a credit score. Most of us also have no idea of what our credit score actually is or how widely it is used. Your credit score is a number between 300 and 850 that is calculated from information in your credit report. Higher numbers are better than lower numbers. Today, whether or not you get credit and how much interest you will be charged if you do get credit are both based on your credit score. The higher your credit score, the lower the interest rate you will be charged on your credit.

Credit scores are used for deciding what your interest rate will be on a car loan or a home mortgage. But your credit score may also be used to decide whether or not you are hired for a job, or how much you are going to pay up for your car insurance. So, it makes sense for you to know what your credit score is.

The 800 pound gorilla of the credit score business is a company called Fair Isaac Corporation. They have an extensive website at the web address of www.myfico.com that discusses how your credit score is calculated and how you can improve your credit score.

The raw materials for calculating your credit score are in your credit report. The information in your credit report is frequently wrong, particularly if you have a common name. You can check the information in your credit report for free once every year at the web address of www.annualcreditreport.com. You should routinely do this. Why should incorrect information in your credit report ruin your credit score?

Your credit score is very important to you. Ideally, you will learn what helps your credit score and what hurts your credit score, and you will try to avoid any actions which would needlessly trash your credit score.

Credit Cards

Credit cards are very handy, but they can potentially do a lot of financial damage. Credit cards can be the crack cocaine of financial security.

If you are carrying a balance on your credit cards, you should try to pay down the credit cards as quickly as possible. As you know, credit card interest rates may start at a low interest rate or even 0%, but can quickly spike up to 18% or more per year. If you have some excess cash, and are looking for a good place to invest, and you are also carrying credit card balances, it is going to be very hard for you to find an investment with a higher risk-adjusted return than just paying down your credit cards.

There are two main theories as to how best to pay off your credit cards. The first theory is that you should just make minimum payments on each credit card and use any excess cash towards paying down your credit card with the highest interest rate. The idea behind the first theory is that this will reduce your credit cards' interest expenses most quickly. The second theory is that you should make minimum payments on each credit card and use any excess cash towards paying down your credit card with the lowest balance first. The idea behind the second theory is you get a sense of accomplishment when you actually pay off a credit card and this makes it more likely you will continue to pay off your remaining credit cards. Use whichever theory makes sense for you.

SPENDING MONEY. WHAT DO YOUR NEED? WHAT DO YOU WANT?

Many people are confused between what you need and what you want. Let's review the basics. You are trying to match up what you need and what you want with oxygen and a new luxury car. Now, let us consider the alternatives. You can have the new luxury car and no oxygen or you can have oxygen and no new luxury car. What do you need and what do you want? You need the oxygen. You want the new luxury car.

So, why do otherwise reasonable people say that they need rather than want a new luxury car? Well, part of it is the marketing efforts by sellers of new luxury cars and every other good and service in our economy. If the hard working marketers can convince you that you need something rather than want something, then you will tend to buy it sooner.

Another reason is what economists call hedonic adaption. When you are used to riding the bus, riding the bus is OK. But, once you get an old used car, then it is hard to go back to riding the bus. Driving an old used car is fine until you get a new economy car. Once you get a new economy car, then it is hard to go back to the hassles of an old used car. Driving the new economy car is fine, until you get a new luxury car. Once you get a new luxury car, then it is hard to go back to the new economy car. In other words, once you get used to something, it quickly becomes a necessity that you now need rather than a luxury that you want.

Under the theory of behavioral finance, going forward from the bus to the old used car to the new economy car to the new luxury car gives you a certain amount of utility or happiness. Also under the same theory of behavioral finance, if you go backwards from the new luxury car to the new economy car to the old used car to the bus, you have a certain amount of negative utility or sadness. The key take away is that the amount of sadness you feel if you go backwards is about twice as much as the amount of happiness you feel from going forwards. This is something you may wish to reflect upon before ramping up your cost of living to an amount that is hard to sustain. If you ever have to go backwards, it is really going to hurt.

So how much happiness do you get from buying things? Well, if you are typical, the short answer is not as much as you think. The happiness you get from buying things tends to fade relatively quickly. The research shows that spending your money on experiences, particularly experiences you plan for far in advance and anticipate such as vacations, sports events, entertainment, etc. appear to give you more long lasting happiness than spending the same amount of money on things. If you are going to increase your happiness by buying things, the research also shows that you will probably have more long lasting happiness if you buy lots of little things rather than one big thing. If you are trying to reduce your current spending, you may wish to consider spending your money less on expensive big things and more on cheaper experiences.

DEBT AND RISK

As you now know, debt is part of the balance sheet. Generally, you take on debt to either buy assets or to pay for expenses. If you take on debt to buy an asset, then you still have the asset, and, initially at least, there is no change to your net worth. On the other hand, if you take on debt to pay for expenses, your net worth is going down. So, generally speaking, you should try to avoid the habit of taking on debt to pay for expenses with no future value.

While I don't want to bore you with a long extended example to prove the point, even if you are buying assets with debt, taking on debt, all by itself increases the risk that something will go wrong in your financial life. If you purchase an asset with a lot of debt, and the value of that asset goes down a little, your net worth is going to go down a lot. For example, if you purchased a house with a really low down payment and a really high mortgage, you are underwater if the value of that house just goes down a little.

Debt, in and of itself, puts risk into your financial life. Therefore, over the long haul, you may want to consider reducing the amount of debt in your life to increase your financial security.

BUYING CARS

Why do we buy cars? Well, getting from Point A to Point B is part of the answer. But, it is a little more involved than that. Each of us probably wants something different from our car. Depending on what you really want from your car, you should probably purchase a different type of car, or maybe not even purchase a car at all.

Consider what you would really want from your car. Personally, I want a car that is red, has two seats, a manual transmission, is fun to drive, and will not likely kill me. I am in the extremely fortunate position of being able to drive the car I want. What if I wasn't? Well then, like any other major purchase, I would just try to buy something where I could spend the least amount of money and get the most utility given my financial situation and goals and dreams.

The two main ways for you to get use of a car are leasing a car and buying a car. Generally speaking, if you plan to use a car for a short period of time, say 2 to 3 years, leasing a car will normally be a better financially for you. On the other hand, if you plan to use a car for a long time, say 7 to 10 years, buying a car will normally be better financially for you.

Please note that if a car manufacturer is desperate to move cars, the manufacturer may offer much more attractive lease terms than is typical to move the cars off their dealers' lots. The classic example of this is leasing luxury cars during a recession at very attractive lease terms. Also, if you lease a car, be sure you understand how many miles you are allowed each year under your lease compared to how many miles you typically drive. The excess mileage charges of a lease can really add up.

BUYING HOMES

Home Ownership

Your home is the biggest source of net worth for the typical household. But, that does not mean that everyone should buy a home.

If you buy and then sell a home, you will pay a lot of transaction costs. Where I live, if you buy a home for $100,000 on Monday, decide to sell it on Tuesday, and on Wednesday sell the home for exactly what you bought it for, $100,000, you would be out about $9,000 in transaction costs such as sales commissions, local taxes, and closing costs. If I buy a publicly traded stock for $100,000 on Monday, decide to sell it on Tuesday, and on Wednesday sell the publicly traded stock for exactly what I bought it for, $100,000, I would be out less than $100 in transaction costs.

Transaction costs are high in buying and selling real estate. The high transaction costs are what makes flipping real estate, that is rapidly buying, fixing up, and selling real estate, extremely difficult even when homes are going up in value rapidly.

Homes are not quick or easy to buy or sell. Another way of saying this is homes are illiquid investments. Buying or selling a home can take a lot of time under the best of circumstances. If you want to sell publicly traded stock and the market is open, you can sell it that day. If you want to sell a home, it can easily take months.

From a financial point of view, there are several benefits to owning your home. First you do not have to pay rent. Second, your home may go up in value. Third, home ownership can act as a forced savings plan for many people.

The cost of renting versus buying varies considerably around the country. In some parts of the country, you will generally be better off financially if you rent. In other parts of the country, you will generally be better off financially if you buy. It all just depends on each area's relationship between the cost of a home and what it costs to rent a similar home both now and in the future.

How much do homes go up in value? The answer depends considerably upon what part of the country we are talking about and what period of time we are talking about. The most unbiased information I can find is the housing data from the Federal Housing Finance Agency. According to this data, over the last 22 years, the average home in the United States has gone up about 3.0% per year. During that same time, inflation in the United States has been about 2.4% per year according to the Department of Labor's all urban consumer price index. So, using the advanced mathematical technique known as subtraction, I calculate that the average home in the United States has gone up in value about 0.6% (3.0% - 2.4%) per year after inflation over the last 22 years. Please note that the operating costs of the average home in the United States can easily exceed 0.6% a year and wipe out this mighty return.

If you want to buy a home only because it might be a good investment, then you need to analyze the geographic area that your home will be in. You also need to consider what is going to happen to that geographic area over the time you will own your home.

What is going to happen to the demand for homes in your geographic area? Are you in an area where more people are moving into as time goes by? Or, are you in an area where people are leaving? What is going to happen to the average household size and the average household income in your area? If the population of your geographic area goes up, the average household size goes down, and the average household income goes up, home prices will likely trend up in your area. On the other hand if the population of your geographic area goes down, average household size goes up and the average household income goes down, home prices will likely trend down in your area.

What is going to happen to the supply of homes in your geographic area? How easy is it for homebuilders to build new homes in your area? Is there available land on which new homes can be built? Does the local government encourage new home construction, or do they make it difficult? If it is easy for homebuilders to build new homes in your area, home prices will likely trend up more slowly than otherwise. If it is difficult for homebuilders to build new homes in your area, home prices will likely trend up more rapidly than otherwise.

What will the federal government do to help or hurt the value of your home in the future? Currently, the federal government is keeping mortgage interest rates near historical lows. This results in lower monthly mortgage payments. If the federal government stops doing this, then mortgage interest rates will trend up, and new buyers of homes will have to pay higher monthly mortgage payments. This will be bad for home prices. Also, currently the federal government indirectly buys almost all of the mortgages that are originated. If the federal government cuts back on these purchases, then mortgages will become less available and cost more. This will also be bad for home prices. Finally, under current tax law you can deduct on your tax return the mortgage interest and the property taxes that you pay on your home. If these tax deductions go away, this will also be bad for home prices

From an investment point of view, when you buy a home you are making a non-diversified, highly concentrated bet on one particular asset that can take a long time to sell and that has high transaction costs to buy and sell. You do not need to buy a home to achieve financial security.

However, in my experience, most people buy a home because they just want to own their own home. For people who just want to own your home my advice is to buy something that you like, try to live in it a long, long time, and try to avoid doing anything stupid when you buy your home.

People want different things in their ideal homes. What is important to you? Try to buy a home that you like. As always, you try to spend the least amount of money and get the most utility given your financial situation and goals and dreams.

Generally, the longer you stay in your home, the better it is for you financially. Given the high transaction costs in buying and selling your home, and the historical rise in home prices, the rule of thumb is that you need to live in your home at least three years just to get back your transaction costs. So, most of the time, if you plan to live somewhere less than three years, renting makes more sense financially for you than buying.

Owning a home can force you to save. If you want to stay in your home, you have to pay your mortgage every month. And, if you pay your mortgage every month and do not refinance, you will eventually own your home free and clear even if saving is hard for you.

Also, if you build up enough equity in your home, you may want to consider a standby home equity line of credit as a good source of emergency funds. A standby home equity line of credit is an agreement you typically make with a bank where you can borrow a certain amount of money against the value of your home if and when you need to. A bank will typically charge you $100 to $200 to set this up for you.

In terms of avoiding doing anything stupid when you buy your home, I highly recommend you make any purchase of your home contingent upon an acceptable to you structural inspection. Homes, even new homes, can have some expensive surprises for their new owners. It is best to know what you are getting into before you actually buy a home.

While your real estate agent may be a lovely person, he or she only gets paid if you buy your home. Therefore your real estate agent might have a financial incentive to recommend a rather easy-going inspector. You, on the other hand, want to choose the toughest, most competent inspector you can find to inspect your future home. If at all possible, you should try to be at the home when your inspector is there. The inspector may communicate more freely to you in person. Most inspectors most of the time will find at least one thing wrong with any home. Making your purchase contingent upon an acceptable to you structural inspection means that you can back out of the home purchase if the inspector finds something wrong.

I highly recommend arranging any financing for your home before you make an offer. You don't want to legally bind yourself to buy something and then find out that you do not have the financing to buy it.

If you have an existing home that you need to sell, depending upon the home buying and selling market conditions, you might be able to get the purchase of your new home contingent on selling your old home. Please note that this is not possible under many market conditions.

If you are buying a vacation home that is located in an area with lots of vacation homes, you also need to think about the economics of vacation home areas. People tend to buy vacation homes when times are good and the economy has been booming for a while. When times are bad and the economy is in recession, lots of people decide to try to sell their vacation home at the same time. When this happens, because times are bad and the economy is in recession, there are normally few buyers for vacation homes. Selling your vacation home in an area with lots of vacation homes can take a much longer time than selling your primary home.

Finally, if you are buying a home with someone you are not married to, I highly recommend that you get a written agreement among all the owners that spells out what happens in the future if someone wants to keep the home, and someone else wants to sell the home. You may want to consider the high transaction costs involved in selling a home when deciding how to value your home in your agreement. If the situation calls for it, you might also want to consider updating your will to reflect your new home ownership.

Mortgages

Homes are highly leveraged investments. The down payment is typically 5% to 20% of your home's purchase price. This means that you will likely get a mortgage to finance the remaining 95% to 80% of your home's purchase price. Generally, the more of a down payment that you can come up with, the less risk it is for your lender to finance your home purchase, and the lower interest rate you will pay on your mortgage. Also, if you are in the situation where you have a choice as to the down payment you can make, remember that the more debt you have the higher the risk that something will go wrong in your financial life.

The mortgage industry is very creative in giving you mortgage alternatives. One alternative you have is whether you pay a fixed interest rate for the entire length of your mortgage or whether you pay an adjustable interest rate for your mortgage.

Generally, the interest rate on an adjustable rate mortgage will be lower than the interest rate on a fixed rate mortgage. This is because an adjustable rate mortgage has less risk for your mortgage lender. The flip side of that is that an adjustable rate mortgage has more risk for you.

You need to understand when the interest rate on an adjustable rate mortgage can go up. Are there limitations on how high the interest rate on your adjustable rate mortgage can go up? If so, what are the limits? What is the benchmark that your adjustable rate mortgage is tied to? Frequently, adjustable rate mortgages have what is known as a teaser rate at their beginning, and the interest rate will go up even if the benchmark stays the same.

A second alternative for your mortgage is how long you will have to repay the mortgage. Historically, the length of a mortgage was 30 years. More recently, 15 year or 20 year mortgages have also become available. The advantage of a 15 year or 20 year mortgage is that if you make the mortgage payments and never refinance, you will own your home free and clear after only 15 years or 20 years rather than 30 years.

Generally, if you get a mortgage with a shorter life than 30 years, your interest rate will be a little less. Of course, the trade-off is that you will lock yourself into a higher monthly mortgage payment. While the monthly mortgage payment will be higher, it might not be as high as you first think. It is generally worth asking your mortgage lender about 15 year or 20 year alternatives just to see what they offer.

It is quite depressing how little of your mortgage payments on a 30 year loan actually goes to reduce the principal balance of your loan in the first couple of years. Even if you decide to go with a 30 year mortgage product, you can still prepay your mortgage by making some additional payments on your mortgage. A small additional monthly payment can dramatically shorten how many years you will need to make mortgage payments.

A third alternative for your mortgage is whether or not you will pay points. In the mortgage world, one point is equal to 1% of your mortgage amount. You pay points upfront to reduce your interest rate on your mortgage loan.

As a rough rule of thumb, if you are going to live in your home for less than three years, then you should go with an adjustable rate mortgage. But, if you are going to live in your home for less than three years, then why are you buying your home rather than renting? If you live in your home for less than three years in most places, most of the time, you will lose money due to the high transaction costs of buying and selling your home.

If you are going to live in your home for more than seven years, it generally makes sense for you to go with a fixed interest rate mortgage. Also, if you are going to live in your home for more than seven years, you really want to consider paying points to reduce the interest rate on your mortgage. The typical person lives in a home for six or seven years, and that is roughly the breakeven time for paying or not paying points on your mortgage loan.

RISK MANAGEMENT PLANNING BASICS

Part of becoming financially secure is trying to reduce the bad things that can happen to you. This is where your risk management planning comes into play. You can be the best investor in the world, but, if you have a huge risk you have not planned for, you could have to cash in all of your great investments to pay for something that goes wrong.

From a theoretical framework, there are four different ways you can manage your risks. First, you can simply avoid the risk. Second, you can transfer the risk by buying some type of insurance. Third, you can try to reduce your risks through noninsurance methods. Fourth, you can retain some or all of your risks.

WHAT RISKS ARE THE MOST IMPORTANT TO PLAN FOR?

I used to sometimes ride my bicycle through traffic to commute to and from my work. There were a number of risks involved in this. One risk is that I would dress inappropriately and maybe get a chill. Another risk was that I would be hit by a car and maybe die or become permanently disabled. Between these two risks, which was my most important risk to plan for? Obviously, it was the risk that I would be hit by a car and maybe die or become permanently disabled.

In risk management planning this is known as the principle of the large loss. The principle of the large loss means that you first want to focus on your risks that are the most important, your risks with big potential losses. You do not focus as much on your risks with small potential losses.

For example, let's apply the principle of the large loss to your health insurance. The big risk is that you will end up in the intensive care unit of a hospital for several days, and have huge expenses that you will need to pay out-of-pocket. The small risk is that you will have to pay another $5 on your co-pay when you visit your doctor. So, when you choose a health insurance policy, if you apply the principle of the large loss, you first want to be sure that you are covered against the big risk with the big potential loss such as paying for the intensive care unit costs. Whether you pay another $5 for your co-pay amount is a small small risk with a small potential loss.

INSURANCE

Insurance is not a way for you to make money. Insurance is a way for you to transfer some of the risk from your life to an insurance company. If you buy insurance and never collect anything from the insurance company that means two good things happened. First, you transferred some of your risk to an insurance company. Second, nothing bad happened to you.

Theoretically, the amount you pay for insurance is the expected value of what the insurance company will have to pay you, plus the insurance company's costs, minus the insurance company's investment income on your premium dollars, plus the insurance company's profits. Every insurance company will have a slightly different calculation of the risk involved in paying you and different expectations about what investment returns they will earn on your premium dollars. This means that different insurance companies will look at your same facts and charge you different amounts for the same insurance coverage. You should take advantage of this by seeing how much different insurance companies will charge you for the exact same amount of insurance.

If you are giving an insurance company money to transfer your risks, you want to make sure that the insurance company is financially solvent enough to actually pay you and make you whole. All insurance companies get a grade for their finances from third party ratings organizations such as the Standard & Poor's, A.M. Best, and Moody's. Obviously, you would prefer to transfer your risk to a financially strong insurance company with a higher grade. Please note that there is a lot of grade inflation in the insurance grading world. You may think that a grade of CCC by Standard & Poor's just means that insurance company is really average. However, that grade is the worst grade that Standard & Poor's gives to insurance companies.

COMMON RISKS AND HOW TO MANAGE THEM

Driving

One way to reduce the risks associated with driving is to avoid driving. You can walk, bike, or use public transportation. However, for many of us, driving cannot be avoided.

There are many noninsurance ways of managing your driving risks. One way of reducing your driving risks is to try to have a safe car. Another way of reducing your driving risks is to drive whatever car you have in a safe manner. Always wearing your seatbelt and shoulder harness is a very good idea. If you have doubts about this, ask anyone who works in the emergency department of a hospital.

Speeding, following the car ahead of you too closely, texting and talking on your phone, and driving while drowsy will all increase the chance that you will be in an accident. Many accidents are also the result of driving while impaired or driving while distracted. So, not driving your car when you are impaired and not driving your car when you are distracted are both excellent ways to reduce your driving risks at no cost to you.

Another way to manage the risks associated with driving is to have car insurance. Most states have a minimum level of car insurance that you must have. For example, in my state, the minimum level of car insurance is liability coverage equal to 25/50/10. What this means in English is that you must have car insurance that pays at least $25,000 to any one person you cause to be injured in an accident, $50,000 to all the people you cause to be injured in an accident, and $10,000 for any damages to any property, like other people's cars, you cause.

The minimum car insurance liability amounts are just that, the minimums. You may want to have way more car liability insurance than the minimums. How much more? Well, that depends on your driving risks, your assets that you are trying to protect, and how much money you have to spend transferring your driving risks to an insurance company by buying car insurance.

Insurance agents and insurance companies have an economic incentive to sell you more, rather than less, insurance than you need. Therefore, the easiest way to get a handle on how much car liability insurance you should have is to contact your insurance agent or insurance company, explain your particular facts, and ask them what amount of car liability insurance they would recommend. Regardless of whether they recommend the state minimum amounts or higher amounts of car liability insurance, you probably will not need any more insurance than what they recommend. Also, if you have more than one car, unless you have some very rare circumstances, your car insurance liability amounts should be the same amount for all of your cars.

In addition to car liability insurance coverage, most car insurance policies also have optional coverage for comprehensive damages and collision damages that generally cover damages to your car. These comprehensive and collision coverages normally have deductibles ranging from $100 to $1,000. If your damage is below the deductible amount, you pay it. If your damage is above the deductible amount you pay your deductible and your insurance company pays the amount over your deductible.

When you spend money on car insurance, the way that you apply the principle of the large loss is to first make sure you have an adequate amount of liability insurance. Your big driving risk with the biggest potential loss that you want to transfer by buying car insurance is the liability part of your car insurance. The amount of your deductible for comprehensive and collision coverage is a relatively small risk with a small potential loss. One way to pay for more liability insurance is to raise your deductible amounts on your comprehensive and collision coverages.

Sickness And Injury

There are many noninsurance ways of managing the risk that we will become sick or injured. For example, most of us are well aware that smoking is not good for you. For someone my age, smoking more than doubles the chance that you will die within the next 10 years. If you are a smoker, quitting smoking would be a great way of managing the risk you will become sick or injured. However, the reality is that cigarettes are highly addictive, and it takes the average person eight or nine tries before he or she can successfully give up the smoking habit. So, if you are a smoker, it may take some time before you can manage your risk this way. But, if you just keep trying to quit, it will eventually take.

Also, what we eat and drink can definitely have an impact on the risk that we will get sick. Generally, eating more fruits and vegetables is definitely good for you.

Another thing that is definitely good for you is getting regular physical exercise. Most of us get woefully little physical exercise. Try to find some physical activities you like and also try to get into the habit of regularly doing the physical activities that you like.

Drinking alcohol is more of a mixed bag. If and only if drinking alcohol does not carry any specific risk for you, moderate social drinking is associated with a longer life.

There was a study out of England of 20,000 healthy adults aged 45 to 79 who were tracked over a long time. The study found that people who did four things lived 14 more years than those who did not do these four things. The four things that were good for your health were do not smoke, eat at least five servings of fruits and vegetables a day, exercise regularly, and drink alcohol in moderation, which the study defined as the equivalent of 1 to 14 shots of liquor per week.

I discuss the study in the class I teach for MBA students. I sometimes worry that the only thing that some of my students will remember decades hence is that I told them the secret to a long life is to line up 14 shots of tequila on the bar every Saturday night and down them all in one go. So, when I discuss the study with my students, I try to emphasize that 1 shot a week is the same as 14 shots a week in the study. I also try to explain that in England drinking is frequently a social activity. So, it is possible that keeping socially engaged, which is also highly associated with a long life, may provide part of the health benefit.

All of the things you previously read about under driving risks will also reduce the risk that you are injured in an accident.

You can also manage the risks of becoming sick or injured by transferring the risk to an insurance company by having health insurance. Most of us get health insurance through our employer. So, we do not have a great deal of choice regarding our health insurance alternatives. If your employer does give you alternatives for your health insurance, you want to remember the principle of the large loss when selecting your health insurance alternative and first transfer the big risks with the big potential losses.

If you work for a large employer, your employer may offer as a fringe benefit a plan variously known as a cafeteria plan or flexible spending account. This plan will let you pay for your out-of-pocket healthcare cost with before-tax dollars by having money taken out of your paycheck. If you know that you will have out-of-pocket health care costs, you may want to consider having money taken out of your paycheck for this type of plan.

The downside of these types of plans is that there is a use it or lose it requirement. If you have money taken out of your paycheck and you do not use it to pay for out-of-pocket health care costs by March 15 of the following year, you lose the money. So, you do not want to have more money taken out of your paycheck than you really anticipate spending on out-of-pocket health care costs.

Where You Live

The risks where you live include the risk of theft, fire, damage and destruction to where you live and your possessions, and the risk that someone will be hurt where you live.

There are many noninsurance ways of managing these risks. You can reduce the risk of theft by trying to live in safer areas, installing better locks on the doors and windows, or installing a burglar alarm.

Becoming Financially Secure

You can reduce the risk of fire by having working smoke detectors. If you have smoke detectors with batteries, you should change the batteries every year on the same day. Many people change the batteries in their smoke detectors on Halloween. Fire extinguishers where you live are also a good idea.

If you live in earthquake country, you may want to consider some simple steps to reduce the damage in the event of an earthquake. For example, strapping your water heater to the wall is an excellent low cost way of reducing the damage an earthquake could cause to where you live.

You can also manage your risks by buying renters insurance or homeowners insurance. Renters insurance is for people who are renting where they live. Homeowners insurance is for people who own the home where they live.

Both of these kinds of insurance cover your liability if the court rules that you caused someone to be hurt where you live. Both of these kinds of insurance also pay you if your possessions are damaged or destroyed where you live. Homeowners insurance also pays you if your home is damaged or destroyed by many, but not all, things. The typical homeowners insurance policy does not cover damages from earthquakes or flooding. Depending on where you live this may or may not be important for you.

How much coverage do you need for your liability if the court rules that you caused someone to be hurt where you live? Again, insurance agents and insurance companies have an economic incentive to sell you more, rather than less, insurance than you need. Therefore, the easiest thing is to contact your insurance agent or insurance company, explain your situation, and ask them what they would recommend. You probably will not need any more insurance than the recommended amount.

If your personal possessions in your home are damaged or destroyed, the renters or homeowners insurance will pay you. However, there are two very different ways that the insurance company will decide how much to pay you. The two types of coverages you can have if your possessions are damaged or destroyed are actual cash value coverage and replacement coverage.

If you have actual cash value coverage and your shirt that cost you $20 is destroyed in a fire, your insurance company will say that the current fair market value of your used shirt is $2, and will pay you $2. If you have replacement coverage and your shirt that cost you $20 is destroyed in a fire, your insurance company will say that they will pay you enough to replace that shirt. So, if it will cost you $25 to get a new shirt to replace your used shirt, the insurance company will pay you $25.

Replacement coverage will only cost you a little bit more in insurance premiums than actual cash value coverage. So, keeping in mind the principle of the large loss, you are typically better off purchasing replacement coverage rather than actual cash value for your possessions as part of your renters or homeowners insurance.

If your possessions are damaged or destroyed, it can be very hard for you to come up with a list of all of your damaged or destroyed possessions for your insurance company. I recommend that you take a video of all of your possessions where you live to help you if you ever need to prove to your insurance company what was damaged or destroyed. Obviously, you want to store this video in a safe place somewhere other than where you live.

If you own your home, homeowners insurance will pay you if your home is damaged or destroyed by many, but not all, things. As you know, for most households the family home is the major source of net worth. Many of these family homes are woefully underinsured.

Remember, you want to enough insurance to pay for rebuilding your home if it is destroyed or damaged. What your home is currently worth is probably not the same number. Also, if you live in an older home, your homeowners insurance may or may not cover the cost to rebuild your damaged or destroyed home to the latest building codes and zoning laws. Your insurance company or insurance agent can tell you what your particular homeowners insurance covers.

Your homeowners insurance policy probably has something called a coinsurance clause buried in the fine print. This coinsurance clause typically states that if you do not have enough homeowners insurance, generally 80% of the value of your home not including the land, then the insurance company is only going to pay part, not all, of your loss from the first dollar of loss onwards. Again, the easiest way to see if you have enough homeowners insurance is to contact your insurance agent or insurance company, explain your situation, and ask them what they would recommend.

Death

We all die one day, but, there is no need to rush things.

The noninsurance ways of managing the risks associated with dying are covered in the parts on managing the risks of driving, and sickness and injury.

You can also help manage the risks of someone depending on you for financial support when you die by buying life insurance.   If no one depends upon you for financial support, there is generally no need for you to buy life insurance.

If you do decide to purchase life insurance, how much should you get? There are rules of thumb that just pull the numbers out of the air that vary between 6 times your earnings to 10 times your earnings. You are better off calculating how much life insurance you should get by looking at what your survivors will need and how much, if any, debt you wish to pay down.

If you are part of a couple where one of you works full-time outside the home and the other stays home and raises small children, you may both need life insurance. The need to replace the income of the person who works full-time outside the home is obvious. Not as obvious is replacing the services of the person who provides childcare but is not paid by anyone for this. It is very hard to simultaneously work full-time outside the home and provide child care for small children. If the person who provides childcare dies, you will need to pay outside childcare providers.

There are a wide variety of life insurance products. At one end of the spectrum is term life insurance, which is pure life insurance. At the other end of the spectrum are permanent life insurance policies, such as whole life insurance, variable life insurance or universal life insurance which have life insurance and also an investment part all rolled into one life insurance policy.

Permanent life insurance policies are sometimes sold to you based upon policy illustrations with rather optimistic hoped for investment return assumptions rather than the actual investment return guaranteed by the insurance policy. Before you purchase any permanent life insurance based upon a policy illustration, you also want to see and consider a policy illustration based upon the policy's guaranteed investment return. Permanent life insurance policies with an investment part are generally not a good deal for you because of modest actual investment returns and high expenses of these types of life insurance policies.

Generally, if you buy life insurance you should stick with term life insurance. If you do decide to buy term life insurance, you may wish to look and see if the policy has guaranteed renewals or conversions regardless of your future health. While you may be in great health now and easily insurable for term life insurance, that might not always be the case.

It is generally cheaper to purchase life insurance as part of a larger group. You may be able to purchase life insurance through your employer. Also, you may be able to purchase life insurance through an organization you belong to or can join such as professional associations, alumni associations or other affinity groups.

Disability
When you are younger, your risk of becoming disabled is actually greater than your risk of dying. Generally, for people who are not yet retired, the risk that you will become disabled is probably the biggest risk that is not being managed.

For most of us who work, the major source of our income is our wages. Under the principle of the large loss, we want to manage the big risk that we will lose that large source of income due to disability and suffer a big loss.

Becoming Financially Secure

The noninsurance ways of managing the risks associated with disability are covered in the parts on managing the risks of driving, and sickness and injury.

There are several insurance ways of managing the risks of becoming disabled. Social Security will pay disability benefits to you if you cannot do any sort of work for more than 12 months and you have worked for at least 1½ to 9½ years depending upon your current age. Additionally, you can purchase a long-term disability insurance which will typically pay you up to 60% or 70% of your current earnings from employment.

If you decided that you need life insurance, you also probably need long-term disability insurance. Additionally, some people who do not need life insurance will need long-term disability insurance.

Ideally, your long-term disability insurance will have the following policy features. It will use a your own occupation definition of your disability where you are considered disabled if you cannot work at your normal job rather than at any job. The coverage will begin three months after you are disabled. The coverage will continue until you are eligible for Social Security.

Realistically, if you purchase long-term disability insurance it is very unlikely you will have all of these ideal policy features. Long-term disability insurance tends to be expensive and hard to get. You normally have to settle for whatever long-term disability insurance policy, if any, that is available to you and reasonably priced.

Like life insurance, long-term disability insurance is generally cheaper to purchase as part of a larger group. You may be able to purchase long-term disability insurance through your employer. Also, you may be able to purchase long-term disability insurance through an organization you belong to or can join such as professional associations, alumni associations or other affinity groups.

If you purchase long-term disability insurance through your employer, try to purchase your long-term disability insurance with after-tax rather than before-tax dollars. This is opposite the way you want to purchase most of your fringe benefits from your employer. If you purchase your long-term disability insurance through your employer with after-tax dollars, you will not pay any income tax on any disability payments paid to you. As you can typically only purchase disability insurance coverage up to a maximum of 60% to 70% of your current earnings, it would be good if you did not have to pay income tax on any disability payments paid to you. This would leave you more money after-tax to pay for your costs of living.

Long Term Care

When you are older and retired, the risk that you will be unable to pay for long-term care in a nursing home is probably the biggest risk that is not being managed by most people. Roughly one in four people who are age 65 will spend at least 12 months in a nursing home. In the area where I live, long-term care in a nursing home costs approximately $6,000 to $8,000 per month.

Medicare is a government sponsored insurance that covers at least some of the healthcare costs of most everyone age 65 and older. But, Medicare will only pay most of the first 20 days of long-term care in a nursing home, and part of the next 80 days of long-term care in a nursing home. After 100 days, Medicare will typically not pay for any long-term care in a nursing home.

Medicaid, not Medicare, is a different government sponsored insurance most everyone age 65 and older can also potentially use to pay for long-term care in a nursing home. However, Medicaid will only pay for long-term care in a nursing home once a person is pretty much broke. So, if you are pretty much broke, you do not really need to worry about paying for long-term care in a nursing home. Medicaid will pay for your long-term care in a nursing home.

You also do not need to worry as much about paying for long-term care in a nursing home if you have a substantial liquid net worth because you can, if necessary, actually pay the $6,000 to $8,000 per month cost out of your net worth.

The people who really need to manage the risk of paying for long-term care in a nursing home are people who have some assets, but not enough assets to pay the $6,000 to $8,000 monthly cost.

You can manage this risk by buying a relatively new type of insurance called long-term care insurance. Obviously, if you choose to purchase long-term care insurance, you want to purchase it from a very highly rated insurance company that has the financial wherewithal to actually pay for any long-term care decades in the future. In recent years, many insurers have quit writing new long-term care insurance policies as their past actuarial assumptions were overly optimistic and they were losing lots of money on these policies.

Typically, people do not purchase long-term care insurance before they are at least 50 years old. Long-term care insurance is insurance is generally cheaper to purchase as part of a larger group. You may be able to purchase long-term care insurance through your employer or an organization you belong to or can join such as professional associations, alumni associations or other affinity groups.

Personal Liability

If you are financially secure or have a large net worth, there is always a very small but real chance that even if you already have the maximum liability coverage offered under your car, renters, or homeowners insurance policy, one day a court will rule you liable for some damage that is larger than your liability coverage of your car, renters or homeowners insurance policy.

If this is a concern for you, the easiest way for you to manage this risk is to transfer the risk to an insurance company by buying a personal umbrella liability insurance policy. Generally, you can buy $1 million to $2 million of additional coverage for approximately $200 to $400 per year per million dollars of coverage.

How can the insurance company offer such a large amount of insurance coverage for such a modest insurance premium each year? First, the risk that the insurance company will actually need to pay on your policy is very small. The personal umbrella liability insurance policy only comes into play once you have exceeded the liability coverage under your car, renters or homeowners insurance policies which are typically required to be set at the highest amount available.

Also, if you read the fine print in your personal umbrella liability insurance policy, you will find that there are many things that are not covered. What if something you want to be covered is not covered? Look for a personal umbrella liability insurance policy from a different insurance company. Each insurance company views your facts differently, and it is possible that at least one insurance company would be willing to write the coverage you want.

It would also be a good idea to have the same insurance company for your car, renters, or homeowners insurance, and personal liability insurance policies. If you do this, only one insurance company is responsible for defending you in court, and there is no possibility of any future finger-pointing among insurance companies as to who must defend you.

RISK PLANNING SUMMARY

Your life has risks. If you want to become financially secure, you need to manage your risks or rely upon divine intervention or good luck. I suggest managing your risks. There are four different ways of managing your risks. First, you can simply avoid the risk. Second, you can transfer the risk by buying some type of insurance. Third, you can try to reduce your risks through noninsurance methods. Fourth, you can retain some or all of your risks. Under the principle of the large loss you want to figure out what are the big risks in your life with the big potential losses and manage those risks first.

Theoretically, where you have unlimited money to spend on managing your risks, you first manage your risks by avoiding the risk and managing the risk through noninsurance methods. Then, for risks that you did not want to retain, you transfer those risks by buying whatever insurance you want.

Practically, where you have limited money to spend on managing your risks, you also first manage your risk by avoiding the risk and managing the risk through noninsurance methods. Then, with whatever amount of money you have to spend on insurance, you transfer the biggest risks with the biggest potential losses in your life by buying insurance.

A cheap source of insurance may be your employer or an organization you belong to or can join such as professional associations, alumni associations or other affinity groups. Also, if you purchase more than one type of insurance from the same insurance company you may qualify for a 5% to 10% discount on all of your insurance policies.

WHAT IS THE POINT OF INVESTING?

The point of investing is to grow your money over time to achieve financial security and your goals and dreams. Ideally, if you invest well over time, you will not have to go to work on Monday morning because you can send your money out to earn money for you on Monday morning while you do something else.

HOW GOOD IS THE AVERAGE INVESTOR?

How good is the average investor? In a word, terrible.

Every year, a financial organization called Dalbar does a study called the Dalbar Quantitative Analysis of Investor Behavior. This study compares how real investors making real investments actually do compared to their investment benchmarks.

For the 20 year period ending in 2012, an investor who invested in the United States stock market benchmark of the Standard & Poor's 500 index would have earned 5.78% a year after inflation. If this same investor invested $10,000 in the stock market benchmark 20 years ago, this amount would have grown to $30,766 after inflation.

How did real investors making real investments in stock mutual funds that invest in the United States stock market actually really do over 20 years? Not so good. The real average investor only earned 1.82% after inflation a year. The real average investor who invested $10,000 20 years ago grew that amount to only $14,344 after inflation. This is a whopping underperformance of 3.96% a year or $16,422 after inflation on each $10,000 invested over 20 years.

This variance from the benchmark by 3.96% a year over a 20 year period is impressive. You do not accomplish this variance with luck. It takes skill. Well, perhaps skill is not the best word. Anyway, how did this happen? Why are most of us such terrible investors?

Well, it turns out that what most of us do is buy an investment when the investment is hot, has already been going up in value for a while, and the price is high. After this, what generally happens is the previously hot investment tends to go down in value for a while due to reversion to the mean. Reversion to the mean is where investment returns tend to move in the direction of their long-term average. So, if an investment has been really hot for a while, it then tends to do worse for a while. Now, you would think that if an investment was a good deal when the price was high, it would be an even better deal when the price was lower, and that most investors would buy even more of it when it went down in price. But, that's not the way most of us really invest.

What most of us do when this previously hot investment goes down is sell the previously hot investment. This is called buying high and selling low and is not a good way to make money. What do most of us then do with our remaining investment proceeds after we sell low? Exactly the same thing we did before, buy the latest hot investment that has been going up in value for a while, with the same results over and over. This is how most real investors making real investments accomplished their really terrible investment returns over the last 20 years.

But, you do not have to be a terrible investor. If you follow the investing principles laid out in this book, you will be a way better investor than most.

THE HARDEST PART OF INVESTING

Here is what is not hard about investing, making a $1 million return on $10 million of investments. Given enough time and due to the miracle of compounding, that is pretty easy and straightforward. Here is what is hard about investing, getting together that first $1,000 or first $10,000 to begin your investing.

So, how do you get together that first money to begin your investing? Think back to the income statement. If you want to get together that first money to begin investing, you have to either increase the amount of income or increases in wealth, reduce the amount of expenses or decreases in wealth, or both increase the income or increases in wealth and also reduce the expenses or decreases in wealth. There really is no other way.

For this reason alone, you probably do not want to get in the habit of spending all the money that you make on your lifestyle costs. Because, if you do spend all the money you make, you will never be able to get together that first money to begin investing and you will always have to go to work every Monday even if there are things you would rather do.

INVESTMENT RISK AND INVESTMENT RETURN

When we talk about investments, risk generally means the risk that your investments will go down in value. Return generally means how much your investments go up or down in value. A very key point is that in the investment world, risk and return are joined at the hip. If you want or need low risk in your investments, then you will generally have to settle for low returns. On the other hand, if you want or need to get higher returns from your investments, then you will generally have to accept higher risk. This is the constant trade-off between investment risk and investment return.

When you invest with a broker, you normally are asked to take some sort of risk preference quiz to determine how you feel about risk, or just state how you feel about investment risk. What is important is how much risk you really can actually take, not how much risk you think you should take. In our culture, we tend to glorify risk takers. Even though you can kid yourself and others about how much risk you are comfortable with, do not do this.

There are number of great sayings about investing. One of my favorites is "if you don't know who you are, investing is an expensive way to find out." What this means is that if you kid yourself and others about how much investment risk you are comfortable with and make the mistake of taking on more investment risk than you should, you normally figure out your mistake at the worst possible time. The worst possible time is when your investments have gone way down in value and you finally admit you cannot take as much investment risk as you hoped you could, and you sell your investments at a big loss. It is extremely important to be honest about how you really feel about risk before you invest to keep this from happening. Remember, most of us have a risk-averse risk preference.

Becoming Financially Secure

When you consider the trade-offs between risk and return, you should first decide what level of investment risk you can really take, not what amount of investment return you need.

After you decide what level of investment risk you are comfortable with and can really take, you can then determine what sort of investment return is typically associated with that level of risk. In the rare case when the investment return typically associated with that level of risk is enough to get you to financial security or your goals and dreams, great, you are done.

In the more common case, where you first decide what level of investment risk you can really take, and then determine that the investment return typically associated with that level of risk is not enough to get you to financial security or your goals and dreams, then you have a tough decision to make. On the one hand, you can increase your investment risk beyond the point you are totally comfortable with. On the other hand, you can accept the lower investment return and figure out how to get by with less money for your goals.

You are the best person in the entire world for deciding how to make this trade-off. No outside financial expert can understand how you value the trade-off as well as you can. Just don't ever kid yourself about how much investment risk you are comfortable with and can really take. It will only end badly.

There are some rare exceptions to investment risk and investment return being joined at the hip. One exception is if you are paying a high rate of interest on some credit card debt. If you pay down some of that credit card debt as an investment, you can avoid the high interest rate on the credit card debt you would otherwise pay. Conceptually, this is like making an investment and getting an investment return equal to the interest that you now do not have to pay. The risk associated with this transaction is zero. If you pay down your credit card, you will avoid future interest payments. So, paying off credit card debt with a high interest rate can be a rare exception of an investment with high return and no risk.

Another rare exception is if you work for an employer who matches your contributions to your 401(k) plan. If you are fully vested in your 401(k) plan, then any amount your employer matches is another rare exception to investment risk and investment return being joined at the hip. For example, if you are fully vested in your 401(k) plan, and your employer agrees to match 50% of whatever you put into your 401(k) plan up to the first 6% of your salary, then the first 6% of your salary that you contribute to your 401(k) plan will have an immediate 50% return from your employer's contribution. Again, this can be a rare exception of an investment with high return and no risk.

HOW DO YOU GET GOOD INVESTMENT RETURNS?

In the 1980s, researchers tried to determine why some investors got better investment returns than other investors. The researchers looked at three potential causes of good investment returns.

The first potential cause of good investment returns was asset allocation. Asset allocation is how you broadly divide your investments among various asset categories. For example, an asset allocation might be 60% of your investments in stocks and 40% of your investments in bonds.

The second potential cause of good investment returns was market timing. Market timing is when you buy or sell a broad asset category such as stocks, based on whether you think that asset category is going to go up or down in the future.

The third potential cause of good investment returns was security selection. Security selection is when you decide which individual investment security to buy or sell based on whether you think that security is going to go up or down in the future. For example, you decide that now is a good time to buy or sell Google stock.

It turns out asset allocation causes more than 90% of good investment returns. So, if you want to get good investment returns, asset allocation is what you need to spend your time and energy on, not market timing, and not security selection. What is wrong with trying to time the markets? Well, theoretically it is a great idea. The problem is that apparently no one can consistently do it in reality. What about security selection? After all, that is what investment magazines and TV shows typically talk about. Well, it turns out it's not really that important. What matters in investing is asset allocation, asset allocation, asset allocation.

SOME ASSET CATEGORIES

So, if asset allocation among asset categories is the way to get better investment returns, what are the asset categories that we allocate among? Well, everyone agrees that there are at least three asset categories, cash, bonds, and stocks. It is very much an open question as to what additional asset categories, if any, you should also include in your asset allocation. The additional asset categories that I am going to mention in this book are real estate, precious metals and collectibles, and alternative investments which are more commonly known as hedge funds. There are more asset categories out there. However, these are the additional asset categories that I think are probably most relevant for you.

It is also very much an open question as to how much, if any, you should further subdivide any of these asset categories in your asset allocation. For example, do you just want to have stocks as the asset category, or do you want to further subdivide the stocks asset category into subcategories? For example, do you want to subdivide the stocks asset category into the subcategories of United States stocks and non-United States stocks? Deciding whether you should subdivide each asset category really depends on how much money you are investing. If you are trying to decide where to allocate a $3,000 IRA contribution, a general asset category of stocks is fine. On the other hand, if you're trying to decide where to allocate $3 million of investments, you may want to subdivide up the general asset category of stocks.

Cash

Some examples of cash as an asset category include bank accounts, certificates of deposit, and money market funds. As an asset category, cash has very little risk. There are little to no fluctuations in price. However, because the risk of cash is low, the return of cash is also low. Historically, over very long periods of time, returns on the cash category have been 0.8% more than the inflation rate. Today, the rates of return on cash are much lower than this.

Cash is a great place to put any funds that you may need on short notice. For example, if you have an actual emergency fund, that emergency fund should be in cash. You are not sure when, if ever, you will need to fund an emergency. Cash is also a great place to put any funds that you are saving up for a big purchase within the next couple of years. In both of these cases, your money in cash will be safe, stable in value, and available to you on very short notice.

Bonds

A bond is where you loan money to some corporation or government. You generally get paid interest periodically. The amount of interest you get paid depends upon the overall interest rates and how risky your bond is compared with other bonds. When the bond matures or ends, you generally get repaid the amount you have loaned.

Historically, over long periods of time, the returns on bonds have generally been higher than the returns on cash because bonds are riskier than cash. Historically, returns on bonds over very long periods of time have been about 2.5% more than the inflation rate. These returns have varied considerably over the years. The main risks of investing in bonds are first, the credit risk that you may not get repaid part or all of the money you have loaned, and second, the purchasing power risk that you will get repaid the money you have loaned, but, due to inflation being higher than you anticipated, the money that you are repaid buys a whole lot less than what you thought it would when you bought the bond.

You can subdivide the asset category of bonds many different ways. I am going to comment on three different kinds of bond subcategories, regular US government bonds, US government bonds that are inflation protected, and US investment grade corporate bonds. Please note that there are a wide variety of other subcategories of bonds out there, but, these are probably the three most relevant subcategories for you.

Regular US government bonds have historically been viewed as the safest investment in the world. The US government has a flag. The US government has a national anthem. More importantly, the US government has a big printing press to print more US dollars any time it wants, a fair court system by world standards, and a long history of paying its debt.

When you buy a US government bond you are buying an investment with historically no credit risk. For US investors, the only risk in buying a US government bond is the purchasing power risk that inflation will be higher than you anticipated, and the money that you are repaid buys a whole lot less than what you thought it would.

When investors are afraid around the world, they tend to buy US government bonds. Typically, US government bonds are used in your investments to serve as an ultra-safe investment and as a hedge against financial reversals in other asset categories.

Regular US government bonds that are not inflation protected, like almost all the bonds in the bond market, pay you a certain fixed amount of interest every year, for example, 3% interest every year. US government bonds that are inflation protected have all the advantages of a US government bond, but, in addition, also have no purchasing power risk. A US government bond that is inflation protected generally pays you a fixed rate of interest plus whatever inflation is while you own it. For example, a US government bond that is inflation protected may pay you 1% per year plus whatever inflation is that year.

Since the same US government is issuing massive amounts of both regular US government bonds and US government bonds that are inflation protected, you can, if you wish, do a simple calculation to see what the bond market is forecasting the future inflation rate will be. For example, if the interest rate on a regular US government bond with a ten year maturity is trading for an interest rate of 3%, and the interest rate on the US government bond with a ten year maturity that is inflation protected is trading for an interest rate of 1%, then subtracting the 1% from the 3% leads us to the conclusion that, on that day at least, the US government bond market is forecasting a future inflation rate of 2 % over the next 10 years.

Becoming Financially Secure

In my example, if you are of the strong opinion that the actual inflation rate will be higher than 2% over the next 10 years, you would buy US government bonds that are inflation protected. If you are of the strong opinion that the actual inflation rate will be lower than 2% over the next 10 years, you would buy regular US government bonds. If you do not have a strong opinion one way or the other, you would buy a mixture of both regular and inflation protected US government bonds.

Another type of US government bond that is inflation protected and is only available to people is the Series I US savings bond. The Series I US savings bonds have some advantages over US government bonds that are inflation protected. First, like all US savings bonds, you typically are not taxed on any of the income until you cash the bond in. Second, once you have owned the bond at least 12 months, you can cash in the bond whenever you want.

The interest a Series I US savings bond pays you is a fixed rate of interest plus whatever inflation is each year. For example, a Series I US savings bond may pay you 1% per year plus whatever inflation is each year. Effectively, what you end up with is a no-cost tax-deferred bond with no credit risk and no purchasing power risk with a put option to sell the bond back at any time you want after 12 months. This is pretty swift from a financial engineering point of view.

You can purchase up to $10,000 per year per Social Security number of Series I US savings bonds. However, currently the interest rate on Series I US savings bonds is a pitifully low 0% plus the inflation rate. Yes, that is correct. It really is 0%. At the current interest rate, these bonds are definitely not a great investment. However, if that 0% ever gets up to 2% or 3% more than the inflation rate, you should consider adding the Series I US savings bonds to the bond part of your investments.

Also, before you purchase any US government bonds that are inflation protected, you may wish to ponder for a while that the same US government that agrees to pay you a fixed interest rate plus the inflation rate also calculates what that inflation rate is every year. There are many different ways to calculate inflation.

I am not saying that the US government will necessarily pull any shenanigans. I'm just saying that it certainly could if it wanted to.

US investment grade corporate bonds are typically bonds with a fixed rate of interest that are issued by US corporations with higher credit ratings. US investment grade corporate bonds are typically graded by third party ratings agencies, like Standard and Poors or Moodys. US investment grade corporate bonds are graded more highly than junk or high-yield bonds. Different third party ratings agencies use slightly different grades. Under Standard and Poor's grading, investment grade bonds are rated BBB or any grade that starts with the letter A. Under Moody's grading, investment grade bonds are rated Baa or any grade that starts with the letter A.

Because US corporations regardless of their credit ratings do not own printing presses to print their own United States dollars, US investment grade corporate bonds are generally considered riskier than the US government bonds. Because US investment grade corporate bonds are generally considered riskier than US government bonds, the interest rates on US investment grade corporate bonds are generally higher than the interest rates on US government bonds.

Conceptually, the key question is whether or not the higher interest rates on US investment grade corporate bonds are high enough to compensate you for the additional risks that you are taking by purchasing US investment grade corporate bonds instead of a US government bonds. The additional risk that you are taking with US investment grade corporate bonds is the credit risk that you will not be repaid part or all of the money that you have loaned. Another unique risk of US investment grade corporate bonds risk is that corporations frequently have the option, but not requirement, to redeem your bonds earlier than is otherwise agreed upon. Corporations will typically only redeem your bonds early when it helps the corporation and hurts you, the bond investor.

The mainstream investment-world view is that US investment grade corporate bonds are a good investment and a good way to diversify the risks of stocks in your investments. This is definitely not the mainstream investment-world view, but I have a personal view that US investment grade corporate bonds do not currently pay you enough additional interest to compensate you for the additional risk of owning them compared to US government bonds.

Because of the high costs in buying and selling individual bonds, the conventional wisdom is that you generally want to purchase your bonds by buying a mutual fund or an ETF that owns bonds until the bond part of your investments is at least more than $100,000.

Also, as an alternative to actually purchasing any bonds, you may want to consider prepaying your debts. Conceptually, you will get a bond-like return on prepaying your debt equal to the interest you now do not have to pay. For example, let's say you have a debt, like a mortgage loan, or a student loan on which you are paying interest of 6%. If you prepay part or all of that debt, conceptually, you are receiving a 6% return. In my example, the 6% return has no risk, because you will save interest at a 6% rate for everything you prepay on the debt. In the current investment climate, a 6% return with no risk is nothing to sneeze at.

Please note that before you do prepay your debts, you want to make sure that after you prepay your debts you will still have enough cash and liquidity in the future. So, for example, if you are prepaying your mortgage, you may want to at the same time arrange a standby home equity line of credit to reborrow part of the equity in your home if it becomes necessary for you to do so.

Stock

Stock is ownership in a company. The investment returns from a stock investment are potentially the payment of dividends, and potentially an increase in the price of the stock. Historically, over long periods of time, compared to the asset categories of cash and bonds, stocks have had the highest risk and the highest return. Historically, over very long periods of time, stocks have had a return of approximately 6.5% more than the inflation rate. Please note that this rate of return has varied even more considerably than bonds depending upon the time period. Stocks go up and down in value a lot.

You can subdivide the asset category of stocks many different ways. I'm going to comment on three different kinds of stock subcategories, US stocks, foreign developed market stocks, and the foreign emerging market stocks. Please note that there are a wide variety of other subcategories of stocks out there, but, these are probably the three most relevant subcategories for you.

US stocks are your default asset category of choice if you are a longer term investor looking for higher returns and willing to accept higher risk. US stocks are a core part of most investments. The US stock market is large, liquid, stable, and, by world standards, a relatively well-regulated market.

Most US investors have more of their stock investments in the US stocks and less of their stock investments in foreign stocks than the research indicates that they should. Most investors around the world, including US investors, tend to overweight their investments with stocks from their own country. This is probably due to investors being the most comfortable investing in stocks of companies they know. However, the US stock market is not even half of the total world stock market capitalization.

What is a reasonable amount of foreign stocks to have? In the past, the rule of thumb, pretty much plucked out of thin air, recommended 20% of your total amount in stocks should be foreign stocks. Currently, another rule of thumb that actually has some research to back it up, recommends approximately 30% of your total amount in stocks should be foreign stocks. Personally, I think you can justify allocating anything between 25% and 50% of your total amount in stocks to foreign stocks depending upon what you are trying to accomplish.

Foreign developed market stocks are stocks from countries with mature economies such as Japan, and Australia, and many countries in Western Europe. Over the long haul, returns from foreign developed market stocks are approximately the same as returns from US stocks. So, why should you invest in foreign developed market stocks? Diversification. Having both US stocks and foreign developed market stocks in your investments together will result in less risk for the same return than just having one or the other asset categories.

Foreign emerging market stocks are stocks from countries with rapidly developing economies such as Brazil, China, and India. Compared to the US stock market, foreign emerging market stocks have a much higher risk. Theoretically, that should also mean that there is also a much higher return over the long haul. Because of the high risk of foreign emerging market stocks, their use, if any, in your investments should be a small percentage of the amount allocated to stocks and foreign stocks.

Real Estate

You can invest in real estate by directly owning real estate. You can also invest in real estate indirectly by owning securities that in turn own real estate.

Directly owning real estate is a good way to get rich slow. The tax treatment of directly owned real estate that you actively manage is fairly good. However, if you directly own real estate, there are some disadvantages. Directly owned real estate tends to be a hassle to manage, illiquid, have high transaction costs to buy and sell, and also tends to have a lot of debt which adds risk.

There is a huge hassle factor in managing directly owned real estate. Your stock or bond investment is not going to call you up in the middle of the night and tell you that there is water gushing from the toilet and ask you what you intend to do about that. The hassles of property management are why most people stop directly owning real estate. Obviously, you can outsource the property management of directly owned real estate, but that means you will have to pay someone to do this.

You can quickly sell most investments with fairly low transaction costs. However, if you want to sell directly owned real estate, you may have to wait months or even years to find someone who wants to buy it. Depending upon the type of real estate, and where it is located, you can easily pay 5% to 10% of the value of the real estate in transaction costs to first buy then sell directly owned real estate.

If you directly own real estate, you will make most of your money on the appreciation in value of the real estate rather than the rental income stream from the real estate. If you decide to directly own real estate, you definitely want to get good tenants who will pay the rent, stay a long time, and not trash your investment. The way to get these good tenants is to be very picky in choosing among your potential tenants. The way to have lots of potential tenants to choose from is to rent out your property at the lower end of whatever the fair market value range is for your rental.

Even though you can have a lot of debt when investing in directly owned real estate, you should try to avoid this. The price of real estate and the rents you can get routinely go up and down. If you have too much debt, you may lose your real estate during one of the inevitable down times because you cannot pay the debt. Always remember when you directly own real estate that it is not how much money you make during the good times that is important. What is important is whether or not you are still solvent at the end of the bad times. Only if you are still solvent at the end of the bad times will you get to enjoy the next inevitable up cycle in your real estate market.

If you want to invest in real estate, but do not want to directly own real estate, you can indirectly own real estate. The investment risks and investment returns of indirectly owned real estate are between the risks and returns of bonds and stocks. You can indirectly own real estate by investing in mutual funds and ETFs that in turn invest in real estate. Also, you can invest in Real Estate Investment Trusts or REITs. Conceptually, a REIT is like a mutual fund that directly owns real estate instead of investment securities.

Like directly owned real estate, indirectly owned real estate is also prone to big cycles up and down. Ideally, you purchase indirectly owned real estate at a time when the price of the mutual fund, ETF or REIT that owns real estate is less than the net asset values of the real estate the mutual fund, ETF, or REIT owns.

Precious Metals And Collectibles

Investments in precious metals, such as gold or silver, or any collectibles such as fine art or beanie babies, are all very similar. All of your investment return is the potential appreciation in price. There is no income part to your investment return. So, if you are going to invest in precious metals or collectibles, you have to consistently be able to time these markets and buy when the prices are low and sell when the prices are high. Realistically, this is impossible for most of us. If you directly invest in precious metals or collectibles, then you also have costs for storing and insuring these investments. If, for some reason, you want to invest in precious metals, but do not want to invest directly, you can invest indirectly by investing in mutual funds and ETFs that in turn own precious metals such as gold or silver.

Alternative Investments (Hedge Funds)

Theoretically, alternative investments or hedge funds can provide high investment returns like you get from stock investments that are not correlated with the returns of other asset categories. Practically, almost no investor should ever invest in alternative investments or hedge funds.

Hedge funds tend to be actively managed. This active management also tends to have high fees compared with other investment categories. The classic fees for an alternative investment or hedge fund is 2% of the assets each year plus 20% of the profits. By way of contrast, the fees for passively managed US stock investments are frequently less than 0.2% of the assets each year and none of the profits.

In most of the publicly available databases of hedge fund returns there is massive survivorship bias. What this means in English is that the hedge funds report their returns during the good years, but do not report returns for the years that they blow up and end. For example, there was a notorious hedge fund in the late 1990s called Long Term Capital Management that, according to the publicly available database of hedge fund returns was up about 32% a year since it began. In reality, this particular hedge fund blew up and ended in a spectacular fashion and lost all of its money in its last year.

In the United States, you can only invest in alternative investments or hedge funds if you are what is known as an accredited investor. An accredited investor meets certain income or wealth standards. For example, a person with income of more than $200,000 per year or $1 million of investable assets will generally be an accredited investor. This means that many of us are not accredited investors and cannot invest in alternative investments or hedge funds. This is a good thing.

Generally speaking, even if you are an accredited investor, the alternative investments and hedge funds available to you are not good investments because of the high fees, potential illiquidity, middling investment returns after fees, and high investment risks for the investment returns you get.

ASSET ALLOCATIONS

The earliest asset allocation advice that I know of is several thousand years old from the Talmud. Translated very freely I believe it says "let every man divide his money into three parts, and invest a third in land, a third in business and a third let him keep in reserve." Presumably, a modern equivalent would be a third in real estate, a third in stocks, and a third in cash and bonds.

More recently, there was a rule of thumb that each year you subtracted your age from 100 and the resulting number was the percentage of your investments to invest in stocks. Your remaining investments are then invested in bonds. So, for example, if you are 57 years old you would subtract 57 from 100 and get 43. Under this rule of thumb, you would invest 43% of your investments in stocks and the remaining 57% of your investments in bonds.

Today, you can access detailed information about the risk and return of various asset allocations. One of the easier websites for most of us to access is the Vanguard website. Currently, the web address is https://personal.vanguard.com/us/insights/saving-investing/model-portfolio-allocations. Websites tend to change, so if this web address does not work, you can search for the phrase portfolio allocation models on the Vanguard website.

If you take a look at these straightforward stock/bond allocations, you will quickly notice a pattern. The pattern is that the higher the percentage of your investments that are invested in stocks, the higher the average yearly return is for that asset allocation.

But, asset allocations do not give you steady returns year after year. For example, the United States stock market has a long-term yearly average return of about 10% before inflation.

But, about four years out of five, the United States stock market's actual yearly return is either a loss or greater than 12% before inflation.

Now, many people only focus on the average yearly return. However, you now know that you should look at the risk of an asset allocation first and only then look at the return of that asset allocation. Before choosing any asset allocation, you need to be very sure that you can live with the amount of risk associated of that asset allocation.

You must hold your asset allocation in good times and in bad times to get the long-term average yearly return of that asset allocation. Times when most people believe that you should cash in all of your investments, and wait for the investment markets to recover. Times when many people believe only fools and morons would ever hold a consistent asset allocation. If your asset allocation has too much risk for you, it will be very hard for you to hold the asset allocation during the inevitable bad times.

At the time of this writing, the Vanguard website showed that for an asset allocation of 60% stocks and 40% bonds the average yearly return was 8.7% before inflation over 87 years, the best year's return was up 36.7% before inflation, the worst year's return was down 26.6% before inflation, and in 21 of 87 years, the asset allocation as a whole was down.

If you are considering this particular asset allocation for you a way to achieve your financial security or goals and dreams, you should first look at the risk of this asset allocation. Only if you are really and truly comfortable with the risk of this asset allocation should you look at the return of this asset allocation. The risk of this asset allocation is that it could go down 26.6% before inflation in any year, and also will probably go down about one out of every four years on average. If you cannot live with this risk, then you should choose an asset allocation with less risk.

HOW TO BUY ASSET CATEGORIES

Active Versus Passive

Active investing is where you invest to try to beat the market. Passive investing is where you just try to get the average market return typically represented by some sort of a market index. For example, if your market is the US stock market, an active investor will try to get a return better than the S&P 500 index or some other US stock market index. A passive investor will just try to get a return equal to the S&P 500 index return or some other US stock market index. Somewhat surprisingly, it turns out that it is really hard to consistently beat the market over time. It's very easy to figure out which active investor has done this in the past over the last five or 10 years. It's very hard to figure out which active investor will do this in the future over the next five or 10 years.

You should buy passive investments rather than active investments for most or all of your investments. The way you buy passive investments is to buy a mutual fund or ETF which in turn invests in the index you want. You want to avoid buying passive investments with high operating costs or passive investments that charge you a load or upfront sales charge.

Mutual Funds

Mutual funds are a great way to buy investments. Mutual funds are not a separate asset category. Mutual funds are a way to own various asset categories. For example, you may buy a mutual fund that in turn invests in a US stock market index, or you may buy a mutual fund that in turn invests in the regular US government bonds market.

Mutual funds offer several advantages. You can get instant diversification with even a small amount of money. You can generally cash in your investment at any time. You get professional management of your investment. Investing in a mutual fund is a great way to make regular smaller investments.

There are also some disadvantages to owning mutual funds. Those professional managers want to get paid. So mutual funds have expenses. Also, you must pay taxes on your share of the mutual funds taxable income, even if you did not sell any of your mutual fund shares.

ETFs

ETFs or Exchange Traded Funds are also a great way to buy investments. Like mutual funds, ETFs are not a separate asset category. ETFs are a way to own various asset categories. Like a mutual fund, you may purchase an ETF that in turn invests in the US stock market or you may purchase an ETF that in turn invests in the regular US government bonds market. Conceptually, you can think of an ETF as a mutual fund that trades on the stock market like a stock.

Compared to its equivalent mutual fund, an ETF will generally have slightly lower costs and slightly less taxable income than its equivalent mutual fund. Historically, because ETFs traded on the stock exchange like a stock, you had to pay a commission every time you bought or sold an ETF. So, historically, ETFs were recommended for big one-time purchases of investments rather than small ongoing purchases of investments. However, currently the major retail discount brokerages, such as Vanguard, Charles Schwab, and Fidelity let you buy or sell at least some ETFs without paying any commissions.

Today, when you are deciding between investing in a mutual fund or the equivalent ETF, the first question to ask yourself is whether or not you will be charged commissions if you buy or sell the ETF. If you will be charged commissions on the ETF, then generally you will invest small dollar amounts in the mutual fund to avoid the commissions on the ETF, and you will generally invest large dollar amounts in the ETF to take advantage of the slightly lower expenses and slightly less taxable income of the ETF. If you will not be charged commissions on the ETF, then generally you will invest both small and large dollar amounts in the ETF.

A PRACTICAL GUIDE TO BEING A GOOD INVESTOR

If you want to be a good investor, the first question you need to ask yourself is do you enjoy investing? For most of us, the answer is no.

If you want to be a good investor, but you do not enjoy investing, you need to decide when you will need the money that you are going to invest. If the answer is less than three years, you should just invest the money in the cash asset category. You will not make much, if anything, on your investment. But, you will still have all of your money plus a little bit of interest when you need to spend the money.

If you will need the money that you are going to invest in more than three years, you need to carefully consider what amount of risk and what return makes sense for you and your investments. When you consider the trade-offs between risk and return, you should first decide what level of investment risk you can really take, not what amount of investment return you need. After you decide what level of investment risk you can really take, you can then determine what sort of investment return is typically associated with that level of risk. The web address for the Vanguard portfolio allocation models may be helpful to you in deciding this. In the rare case when the investment return typically associated with that level of risk is enough to get you to financial security or your goals and dreams, great, you are done.

In the more common case, where you first decide what level of investment risk you can really take, and then determine that the investment return typically associated with that level of risk is not enough to get you to financial security or your goals and dreams, then you have a tough decision to make. On the one hand, you can increase your investment risk beyond the point you are totally comfortable with. On the other hand, you can accept the lower investment return and figure out how to get by with less money for your goals and dreams.

Remember, you are the best person in the entire world for deciding how to make this trade-off. No outside financial expert can understand how you value the trade-off as well as you can. Just don't ever kid yourself about how much investment risk you are comfortable with. Again, it will only end badly if you overestimate how much investment risk you can really take.

Your asset allocation does not have to be complicated. It is fine to start out with just two asset categories, stocks and bonds. As the amount that you are investing increases, you may wish to consider adding additional asset categories or subdividing asset categories such as the stocks and bonds.

Once you have decided what your asset allocation is, you can just buy that asset allocation by buying low cost passive mutual funds or ETFs from any reputable discount retail brokerage. Examples of reputable discount retail brokerages are Vanguard, Charles Schwab, and Fidelity. There are many other reputable discount retail brokerages. Vanguard, as well as some of the other discount retail brokerages, has mutual fund selectors and ETF fund selectors on their website that can help you pick your specific mutual funds and ETFs to help you buy your asset allocation.

Finally, you need to reevaluate everything at least once a year. You need to ask yourself at least once a year if you are still comfortable with the amount of investment risk and investment return of your particular asset allocation. Also, you need to do what is known as rebalancing.

Rebalancing is basically getting your asset allocation back to its desired target allocation. For example, if you decided that your target asset allocation is 60% stocks and 40% bonds, and you actually do this, after a year, your actual investments will probably not still be 60% stocks and 40% bonds because the stock markets and bond markets will likely have different returns each year.

So, for example, if, at the end of the year, your actual investments were 62% stocks and 38% bonds, you would rebalance your investments by selling some part of stock investments to take the percentage of stocks down to 60% and purchasing bonds with the sales proceeds to take the percentage of bonds up to 40%. If you do not rebalance at least once every year, you will not have the investment risk and will not get the investment returns associated with your original target asset allocation.

Also, if you are investing money for your retirement, you may wish to consider a type of mutual fund variously known as a target date fund or lifecycle fund. These types of funds normally have your anticipated year of retirement in the name of the fund. For example, the ABC fund family will likely have the ABC 2020 fund for people anticipating retirement in the year 2020. Similarly, the ABC fund family will also have the ABC 2030 fund for people anticipating retirement in the year 2030, and so on. The benefit of a target date or lifecycle fund is that your asset allocation automatically changes as you get closer to your retirement date.

Please note that all target date funds and lifecycle funds are NOT created equal. If you decide to purchase this type of investment, you should look for a fund with low operating costs. Also, funds that have the same retirement year from different fund families can have very different asset allocations. You want to make sure that the asset allocation of any fund you invest in matches your desired level of risk and return.

Finally, please note that you can adjust the investment risk and return of target date funds or lifecycle funds by changing the target year of your retirement. If you want more investment risk and, presumably, more investment return, you can choose a fund with a retirement date later than your actual anticipated retirement date. Similarly if you want less investment risk and, presumably, less investment return, you can choose a fund with a retirement date earlier than your actual anticipated retirement date.

Some of us enjoy investing and want to try to beat the market. If you do enjoy investing and you want to be a good investor, here is what you also need to do. Ask yourself how you are going to invest. If you consistently follow almost any reasonable investment theory, you will be much better off than the people chasing the latest hot investment ideas who end up buying high and selling low.

You also need to ask yourself why you, dabbling on a part-time basis, are going to go head-to-head and win against the cutthroat full-time Wall Street investors with all the latest investment technology. Many of us have been working full-time at what we do for years. You may have considerable education as to how to do your job, and you probably have lots of experience doing your job. What is the chance a Wall Street investor dabbling part-time in what you do for a living could do your job better than you? It's not very likely. Now, why do you think you can beat a Wall Street investor at what they do full-time again?

If you want to try to beat the market, be sure to select an appropriate investment benchmark to check your actual investment results against. If it turns out you are not beating your benchmark after several years, you may wish to consider shifting part or all of your investment assets to another investment strategy such as the one outlined above for people who do not try to beat the market.

RETIREMENT PLANNING BASICS

Unless you plan to die at work one day, you may want to consider some retirement planning. Retirement planning is basically a way of figuring out how you are going to pay for your costs of living when you are no longer working at the day job.

Essentially you can make two mistakes in planning for the finances of your retirement. You can save too much, or you can save too little. Everything else being equal, it is best if you save too much. The main financial risk of retirement is that you will outlive your money.

However, everything else is not equal. When you make a decision to save for your retirement in the future, you are also deciding to not spend money today. So, whatever decision you make between saving money for the future and spending money today is a trade-off. You are the best person in the world for knowing your values, goals and dreams, and then deciding how to make this trade-off.

RETIREMENT PLANNING CALCULATIONS

Retirement planning calculations can get very complicated very quickly. Retirement planning calculators that use some form of probabilistic scenarios will generally give you a better result than calculators that do not. A retirement planning calculator that gives you an answer along the lines of "there is an 83.47% chance that you will achieve your retirement planning goals" is using probabilistic scenarios. Your chance of success is expressed in terms of a probability or percentage that something will happen.

Realistically, most of us should use some sort of reputable online retirement planning calculator to make our retirement planning calculations. Even if you are really good with spreadsheets, you still probably want to use online calculators as it is difficult to do probabilistic scenarios with most spreadsheets.

If you use more than one reputable retirement planning calculator, you will quickly note that you get widely varying answers from each calculator. Why? Basically, while all of the assumptions for each calculator are probably reasonable, those reasonable assumptions tend to be very different from calculator to calculator.

RETIREMENT CALCULATION ASSUMPTIONS

Before you use any of the reputable retirement planning calculators, you need to decide what assumptions are reasonable for you. Once you have decided what assumptions are reasonable for you, you can then try to find reputable retirement planning calculators with the same or similar assumptions to make your retirement planning calculations. Here are some of your more important retirement planning assumptions.

How Many Years Will You Be Retired?

If you postpone your retirement date by one year, this will give you one more year to build up your savings and one less year to draw on those savings. It is common for people to push back the time when they will retire to increase the odds they will have enough money in retirement.

Once you are retired, how many years will you be retired? In other words, what is your life expectancy? Most people think of life expectancy as a single number on a life expectancy chart. For example, currently, the web address for the Social Security Administration latest table of life expectancies is www.ssa.gov/OACT/STATS/table4c6.html. Websites tend to change, so if this web address does not work, you can search for the phrase period life table, 2009 on the Social Security Administration website.

According to this chart, as a 57 year-old male, my life expectancy is 23.61 years. But, that does not mean all of us 57 year-old males currently alive will drop dead in exactly 23.61 years. What this really means is that for all the 57 year-old males currently alive, one-half of us will be dead in 23.61 years. In other words, one-half of all 57 year-old males will live longer than 23.61 years, and will also need to pay for their lifestyle cost for longer than their 23.61 years.

Your own life expectancy will differ from the average life expectancy shown on a life expectancy chart depending upon your family history, healthiness of your lifestyle, and your luck. Even if you have an average family history, healthy lifestyle, and luck, it is prudent for you to plan on living beyond your life expectancy. Remember, one-half of the people will live beyond the average life expectancy.

What Will Be Your Cost Of Living In Retirement?

The starting point of your cost of living in retirement is your cost of living today. What if you have no clue about your cost of living today? Well, that is another good reason to consider tracking your cost of living today as mentioned in the budgeting part of this book.

There is an old rule of thumb that your cost of living when you are retired will be about 80% of your cost of living before you are retired. Like most rules of thumb, this rule of thumb is better than nothing, but can be improved upon. Try to figure out what your actual cost of living in retirement will be rather than just using 80% of your cost of living before you are retired. Also, remember if your retirement is years and years away, your cost of living before you are retired may trend up over time from where it is now as you get used to more expensive things.

Once you retire, some of your costs of living will probably go down, and other of your costs of living will probably go up. For example, your costs of getting to and from work will likely go down. On the other hand, your healthcare costs will likely go up.

I recommend you think of your future retirement cost of living in today's dollars rather than trying to gross them up to future inflation adjusted dollars. If you use today's dollars, it is easier for you to reality check the reasonableness of your cost of living in retirement.

How Will You Pay For Your Cost Of Living?

When you are retired, you will pay for your cost of living by some combination of part-time work, Social Security payments, your savings, and, possibly, a reverse mortgage if you own a home.

Many people plan on working part-time for money to help them pay their cost of living in retirement. There are two major problems with counting on part-time work to pay for some of your retirement cost of living. First, your health may not permit you to work as you have planned. Second, it can be hard to find a job. Many people plan on working part-time after their retirement. However, only about one-quarter of the people over age 65 work for money after their retirement.

Paying for your cost of living with Social Security payments and your savings are discussed later on.

If you own a home and have equity in your home when you retire, it is also possible for you to pay for some of your costs of living with what is known as a reverse mortgage. A reverse mortgages is where you borrow money on the value of your home but do not have to repay any of the borrowed money or interest on the borrowed money until you die. When you die, generally, your home will be sold and the reverse mortgage will be paid off. Generally, if the sale of your home is not enough to repay all of the loan and interest, no one is personally liable for the difference.

You have to be at least 62 to have a reverse mortgage. All the other mortgages on your home have to first be paid off before you can get a reverse mortgage. Your credit rating is fairly irrelevant if you get a reverse mortgage because the lender will look to your age and the value of your home to pay off the reverse mortgage.

Reverse mortgages tend to have lots of fees and relatively high interest rates. The reverse mortgage is not the first place you want to look to for paying your retirement cost of living. However, many people's wealth is in their homes. So, if you want to keep your home when you are retired, and part-time work, Social Security payments, and your savings will not pay for your cost of living, you may want to consider a reverse mortgage.

Social Security?

Under the current rules, generally, if you have worked for at least 10 years, you are entitled to a Social Security payment based on your lifetime wages. Your Social Security payment is paid to you every month when you are retired, goes up every year for inflation, and is guaranteed by the US Government. If you were born after 1960, you will get your full Social Security payment at 67. If you were born after 1960, you can get 70% of your full Social Security payment at 62, but you will then not get your full Social Security payment at 67. If you were legally married for at least 10 years, you can also get Social Security payments based on your spouse's or ex-spouse's lifetime wages.

Generally, under the current rules, you should begin taking your Social Security payments as soon as you can at 62 if you need the cash now, you do not anticipate living as long as is typical, and/or you think your Social Security benefit will go away or be radically reduced by a law change in the immediate future.

Generally, under the current rules, you should begin taking your Social Security payments as late as you can if you are not yet 65 and still working and your Social Security payments would be reduced if you took them prior to 65, you do not need the cash now, you anticipate living longer than is typical, you do not think your Social Security benefit will go away or be radically reduced by a law change in the immediate future, and/or you like the guaranteed increase of 8% a year in your Social Security payment for each year you wait beyond 62 to take your Social Security payment.

Those are the current rules about Social Security. However, the current rules are highly likely to change before you are retired. The latest calculations show that Social Security will totally run out of money in the year 2033 if no changes are made to the current rules.

So, how much Social Security, if any, are you really going to get? All we can do is guess. Here is my current guess. It is a fact that politicians pay more attention to old people than young people. This is because old people tend to vote more than young people and all politicians like to get elected or reelected. It is also a fact that currently Social Security payments are more than 90% of the total income of about one-quarter of married couples who receive Social Security and about one-half of unmarried people who receive Social Security. Finally, I believe that it is also a fact that if the people for whom Social Security payments are more than 90% of their total income did not receive Social Security, then some of these people would likely starve to death.

I guess, and remember, this is just a guess, that Social Security will survive in some form for at least the poorer and/or older members of our society. I cannot believe that we as a country are going to let grandma and grandpa starve to death. It is the morally wrong and politically stupid. However, I think that the rich and/or younger people of our society should not count on getting any Social Security payments.

How Much Do You Have To Save For Retirement?

Okay, not counting on getting any Social Security payments seems prudent. The problem is, if you won't get any Social Security payments, you will need to save much more money to pay for your cost of living in retirement.

Traditionally, many people used a rule of thumb that said you could take 5% a year withdrawal rate out of what you saved for retirement. For example, for each $10,000 a year of costs of living you needed to pay for with your retirement savings, if you used a 5% a year number, you would have to save $200,000 ($10,000 divided by 5%). You could then spend $10,000 of the $200,000 in the first year on your costs of living and increase this $10,000 by the inflation rate for the rest of your retirement.

More recently, many people have tended to use another rule of thumb that said you can only take 4% a year withdrawal rate out of what you saved for retirement. For example, for each $10,000 a year of costs of living you needed to pay for with your retirement savings, if you used a 4% a year number, you would have to save $250,000 ($10,000 divided by 4%). You could then spend $10,000 of the $250,000 in the first year on your costs of living and increase this $10,000 by the inflation rate for the rest of your retirement.

As you can see, just changing the withdrawal rate by 1% can have a big impact on how much you need to save. So, what is an appropriate withdrawal rate for you to use? That is the subject of much debate and little agreement among retirement planners. My sense of the current conventional wisdom is that if you are going to take out a fixed amount in the first year of retirement and gross up that fixed amount by the inflation rate, then you should use a maximum withdrawal rate of about 4.5%. In other words, for each $10,000 a year of costs of living you want to fund with retirement savings, you will need to save approximately $222,000 ($10,000 divided by 4.5%).

On the other hand, if you are willing to vary the percentage that you can take out of your personal savings to fund your retirement, my sense of the current conventional wisdom is that you can use a higher maximum withdrawal rate of about 5.5%. In other words, for each $10,000 a year of costs of living you want to fund with retirement savings, you will need to save approximately $182,000 ($10,000 divided by 5.5%).

This higher withdrawal rate that you are willing to vary also generally assumes that if the actual withdrawal percentage after investment returns and withdrawals ever creeps up to about 6.6% of your actual remaining savings, you will need to chop your withdrawal for that year by 10% of your pre-existing withdrawal rate. This lower amount then becomes the new amount to gross up by the inflation rate. On the other hand, if the actual withdrawal percentage after investment returns and withdrawals ever goes down to 4.4% of your actual remaining savings, you can increase your withdrawal for that year by 10% of your pre-existing withdrawal rate. This higher amount then becomes the new amount to gross up by the inflation rate.

The latest authoritative study of variable withdrawal rates, in my opinion, is the article Decision Rules and Maximum Initial Withdrawal Rates by Jonathan T. Guyton that appeared in the March, 2006 edition of the Journal of Financial Planning. You can search for this article online, read the detailed analysis and decide for yourself what you think of using withdrawal rates that vary in retirement.

Taxes?

You are still going to have to pay taxes in retirement. How much depends upon the overall tax laws when you are retired, and how your personal situation fits into those future overall tax laws. In other words, it is not easy to forecast. Generally, the overall tax laws will probably require more taxes for most people in the future for the reasons discussed in the taxes part of the book.

What is a little bit easier to forecast is whether you will pay state and local income taxes in retirement. Most states in the United States have some sort of state income tax. If you are a resident of one of the states when you are retired, you will likely pay that state an income tax. Some states, including Alaska, Florida, Nevada, South Dakota, Texas, Washington, and Wyoming do not charge residents state income taxes. Depending on which state and city you live in when you are retired, you may or may not pay state and local income taxes.

HOW TO SAVE FOR RETIREMENT TODAY

401(k) plans and Individual Retirement Accounts or IRAs are both excellent ways to save for retirement. A 401(k) plan is offered by many employers for their employees. If your employer offers you a 401(k) plan, it may also match your contributions. Matching is like free money for you. If your employer offers matching of your 401(k) plan contributions, this is probably the first place you should save for your retirement. If you cannot put as much into your 401(k) plan as you want to today, you may want to consider putting part or all of your future bonuses or raises into your 401(k) plan.

Your employer may have two different kinds of 401(k) plans, a traditional 401(k) plan and a Roth 401(k) plan. The difference between these is that for any amount you contribute to a traditional 401(k) plan you get income tax savings today, but, when you take the money out in retirement, you have to pay income taxes. On the other hand, with a Roth 401(k) plan you do not get any income tax savings today, but, when you take the money out of retirement, you do not have to pay income taxes.

If you think your personal marginal income tax rate will be lower when you are retired than today, you would lean towards the traditional 401(k) plan. If you think your personal marginal income tax rate will be higher when you are retired than today, you would lean towards the Roth 401(k) plan. If you do not have strong opinion one way or the other, either plan, or a combination of both plans, is a good choice for you.

When you leave your old employer, you can easily roll over any amount you have in your 401(k) to your new employer's 401(k) or your own IRA. You should definitely always roll over 401(k) balances. If you take out the money instead and spend it, you will pay a boatload of taxes and penalties on the money you did not roll over.

When you roll over your 401(k), have your new employer or your IRA plan custodian go get your money from your old employer's 401(k) plan. This way, you can be sure that your entire 401(k) amount gets rolled over. If you just ask your old employer for a check for your 401(k) balance, your old employer will withhold 20% of your 401(k) amount and send that off to the Internal Revenue Service as a prepayment of your income taxes and then only give you a check for the remaining 80% of your 401(k) amount. So, if you then roll over that check, you will only roll over 80% and you will be taxed on the remaining 20% that you did not roll over.

IRAs are also a good way for you to save for your retirement. Generally, you can contribute up to $5,500 a year into an IRA or $6,500 a year if you are at least 50 years old by the end of the year. Like 401(k)s, there are two different kinds of IRAs, traditional IRAs and Roth IRAs. Generally, everyone can make a traditional IRA, but, depending on whether you or not you are covered by a 401(k) plan at work, and how much taxable income you have, you may or may not be able to get a tax deduction for a traditional IRA. Also, depending upon how much taxable income you have, you may or may not be able to even make a Roth IRA contribution.

Generally, when you are trying to decide between making a contribution to a traditional IRA or a Roth IRA, you should first ask yourself if your taxable income is too high to make a Roth IRA. If the answer is yes, then your only choice is to either make or not make a traditional IRA contribution.

If the answer is no, then the next question to ask yourself is whether you will get an income tax deduction for your contribution to a traditional IRA. If the answer to that question is no, then your only choice is to either make or not make a Roth IRA contribution.

If the answer to that question is yes, and if you think your personal marginal income tax rate will be lower when you are retired than today, you would lean towards the traditional IRA. If you think your personal marginal income tax rate will be higher when you are retired than today, you would lean towards the Roth

IRA. If you do not have strong opinions one way or the other, either IRA, or a combination of both IRAs, is a good choice for you.

If you want to shift some of the risk you will outlive your money, you may also want to consider buying a low cost annuity from a highly rated insurance company to fund part or all of your retirement cash needs. The advantage of an annuity is that as long as you are alive and the insurance company is solvent, you will receive an annuity payment. If you do decide to buy an annuity, it would be good to get an annuity with a payment that goes up for inflation so you maintain your purchasing power over the years.

WHAT MAKES FOR A HAPPY RETIREMENT?

A happy retirement is much more than getting the finances of your retirement planning right. Most of us have goals and dreams other than just money. Retirement is a chance for you to do things you did not have the time to do when you were working, and to work towards your goals and dreams. Having a great reason to get out of bed in the morning is a good thing. Trying to stay healthy, getting exercise, and having a strong social network of family, friends, and neighbors all increase the odds you will be happy in retirement.

WHAT IS THE GOAL OF TAX PLANNING?

If you ask most people what the goal of tax planning is, they would say the goal of tax planning is to reduce the taxes that you pay. This is wrong.

If you really think after reading this book that the goal of tax planning is to reduce your taxes, you can just loan me $100. If you do this, I promise to never ever repay your loan. You can call me, you can write me, I will not repay your loan. What I will do, since your tax planning goal is to reduce your taxes, is tell you how you can reduce the taxes that you will pay.

Specifically, you can deduct the $100 as a personal bad debt deductible as a short-term capital loss on your tax return. You will then have a $100 loss on your tax return which should save you about $15 to $35 depending on your marginal tax rate. Now, let's step back and look at this. If you loan me money and I do not repay it, you are out $100 in cash and you have reduced the taxes that you pay by a maximum of $35. You are still out-of-pocket at least $65. Is that really what you really want?

So, if the goal of tax planning is not to reduce the taxes that you pay, what is the goal of tax planning? The goal of tax planning is actually to maximize your income, wealth, and utility after you pay all of your taxes. That's it. The taxes that you pay are just another cost of your lifestyle. You should be focused on your income, wealth, and utility after taxes, not on your tax expense.

If you have a chance to get more money, but only on the condition you pay taxes on that money, take the money. You will still end up with more money even after you pay your taxes. Also, you should never spend any money if the only reason you are doing so is that you can deduct the money you spend on your tax return. You will be out more money than your tax savings.

THE BASICS OF THE TAX SYSTEM IN THE UNITED STATES

If you don't like the federal income tax laws in the United States, just wait a little bit, they will change. The tax laws we have in the United States are just a decades-long accumulation of what seemed a good idea at the time for a bunch of politicians in Washington DC.

Politicians everywhere like to be reelected. The politicians in Washington DC are generally at the top of their game and are highly attuned to getting reelected. This includes the politicians constantly tweaking the tax laws in this country to help them get reelected. So, the tax laws in the United States are in a constant state of flux. Despite what the politicians tell you to get elected or reelected, the overall taxes in this country are likely headed up in the coming decades to pay for the enormous projected government expenses.

Here are some of the basics of the federal income tax laws today. But, remember, the tax laws today could change tomorrow.

The federal income taxes that you pay depend upon your marital status on December 31st. For federal income tax purposes you are either single, married and filing a tax return jointly with your spouse, married and not filing a tax return jointly with your spouse, or something called head of household. Whether or not you are married generally depends on the laws of the state that you live in. If you are married to someone of the same gender, some special tax rules may apply to you, and you should probably seek the advice of a qualified tax professional.

If you are married, should you file a tax return jointly with your spouse? Well, like so much in tax, that depends. Very generally, if you live in the community property state or one of you works and one of you does not, you will normally pay less taxes as a couple if you file a tax return jointly with your spouse. Other than that, there are no general rules as to whether you as a couple should file together or separately. You can always calculate your taxes both ways each year and file whichever way saves you in taxes.

A head of household is a single person who generally provides the majority of financial support for a family member who lives in the same home. If your marital status is head of household, you will pay less in income taxes than if your marital status is single.

When you file a tax return each year, you can either itemize deductions or take what is known as a standard deduction. A standard deduction is where you get to deduct a standard minimum amount of itemized deductions even if everyone agrees the reality is you have no itemized deductions. For 2013, the standard deduction for a single person is $6,100 and the standard deduction for a married couple filing jointly is $12,200. Each year, you just take the higher of your actual itemized deductions or your standard deduction on your tax return. This means you get no tax savings from your itemized deductions until the total of your actual itemized deductions are more than your standard deduction amount.

When you are doing your tax planning, you want to pay attention to your marginal tax rate rather than the average tax rate. Your marginal tax rate is how much more in taxes you will pay if you add some additional income to your tax return. If you will never get any Social Security, your marginal tax rate from your wages may be higher than you think. 6.2% of the first $113,700 of your wages is withheld to pay your Social Security taxes. If you never get any Social Security payments, the marginal tax rate on the first $113,700 of your wages is whatever your marginal income tax rate is plus the 6.2% of Social Security taxes that you never got any benefit from.

In recent years, the Internal Revenue Service has dramatically ramped up the information reporting requirements for you if you have foreign bank accounts, foreign brokerage accounts, or get any money from or exercise any influence over any foreign company, partnership, or trust. You do not necessarily need to pay anything more in taxes, but you do need to provide a lot of information reporting. The penalties for not reporting any required information can be draconian. If any of this applies to you, you should definitely seek advice from a qualified tax professional who has other clients in your tax situation.

PREPARING YOUR TAX RETURN

If you have some big numbers on your tax return, or if something about your tax situation is unusual, or if you just want the peace of mind that your tax return is prepared correctly, then you should find a qualified tax professional to help you with your taxes.

A qualified tax professional, in my opinion, is someone who has worked on taxes full-time for a minimum of five years. A professional who does something all the time for long enough, tends to get pretty good at whatever he or she normally does. Where many professionals get into trouble is when they do something they rarely do. So, it is best that the qualified tax professional you choose has many other clients who are in your tax situation.

Inevitably, some people will consider preparing their own tax return using tax preparation software, such as TurboTax. Tax preparation software can work great if you are the person they were thinking of when they designed the software. If you have a W-2, some 1099 forms, and own a house, you are the person they were thinking of when they designed most tax software. On your other hand, if you have a tricky payroll tax situation because you work for an international organization, and one day would like to be the cabinet member in charge of the Internal Revenue Service, you are not the person they were thinking of when they designed most tax software, and you should probably use a qualified tax professional familiar with your unusual tax situation. Otherwise, you may have an embarrassing confirmation hearing.

If you do choose to use tax preparation software, then you just want to carefully answer all questions the tax software asks you. If you don't really know the answer, you should use the help menus and other resources to find out the answer to the question rather than just answering yes or no. All the yes and no answers you input into the tax software are sending you down particular logic trails. You can end up with a very bizarre tax return if you just answer the questions yes or no when you are not sure of the answer.

TAX PLANNING

Employees

If you are an employee, you should take a look at your fringe benefits for your tax planning. Employee fringe benefits are things such as insurance plans or matching of your 401(k) plan contributions that you can get through your employer. Generally, with an employee fringe benefit you get something of value without having to pay any taxes on it. You should periodically check in with your employer to see if it makes sense for you to update your employee fringe benefits.

As an employee, you will be asked to fill out a W-4 form that calculates how much income tax is withheld from your wages. Most people try to just get close. If you like to get a refund, you should enter in fewer exemptions than the calculations show on the W-4 form. If you want to increase your take home pay now and owe taxes later, you should enter in more exemptions than the calculation shows on the W-4 form. You should be aware that if you enter more than nine exemptions, your employer may question you about this. Also if you are married, and if your spouse earns about the same amount of money as you, the exemption calculations on the W-4 form will probably not have enough income tax withheld from your either of your wages.

Debt

You generally cannot deduct interest on debt you got to fund your personal costs of living. You generally can deduct interest on debt you got to buy your home or to buy investments.

Children

Children take a shockingly large number of years to cash flow. As a small help, if your child is less than 17 years old, and if your taxable income is not too high, you can get a child credit of up to $1,000 per child on your tax return.

If you pay for child care out-of-pocket, you can generally get a child care credit of at least $600 per child. If you pay for child care through your employer's dependent care assistance plan, you can generally have up to $5,000 per year taken from your wages and paid to your child care provider without any income tax being charged on this.

Insurance

Generally, when something bad happens and your insurance company pays you money, you do not have to pay any taxes on that money. The one exception to this is if you paid your long-term disability insurance premiums with after-tax dollars rather than before-tax dollars, and if you then receive long-term disability insurance payments, you have to pay tax on the long-term disability insurance payments. This is why you always want to pay any of your long-term disability insurance premiums with before-tax dollars if that alternative is available to you rather than after tax dollars.

Investments

What matters is your investment return after you pay your taxes, not your investment return before you pay your taxes. You should not assume that all of your investments with the same before-tax returns also have the same after-tax returns. Under current tax laws, certain types of income, such as qualified dividend income and long-term capital gains, are taxed at lower tax rates than other types of income such as interest income and short-term capital gains.

If you are trying to decide between investing in an equivalent mutual fund or ETF, in general, an ETF will have a little less taxable income each year than the equivalent mutual fund.

If you have investments in a taxable account, you may wish to consider tax loss harvesting. Tax loss harvesting is when you sell an investment that has gone down in value from when you purchased it, thereby harvesting the tax loss. You then immediately turn around and purchase a similar, but not identical, investment. If you jump through all the tax hoops correctly, you will have a loss to put on your tax return, still own roughly the same investment, and only be out the cost of some commissions.

If you have investments in both taxable accounts and tax-deferred accounts such as 401(k)s and IRAs, there has been considerable debate among tax professionals as to what type of investments you should put where. My sense of the latest thinking is that you want to put investments which generate lots of taxable ordinary income, such as bonds and REITs in your tax-deferred accounts, and also put more volatile lightly taxed investments, such as stocks, in your taxable accounts.

Retirement

The retirement planning part of the book has information on how you can plan for taxes as part of your retirement planning.

WHAT IS ESTATE PLANNING?

We all die one day. Estate planning is deciding what you would like to have happen at the end of your life rather than having other people and/or the courts decide what happens at the end of your life. Things like who will make your healthcare decisions if you are unable to do so, and who gets your assets when you die?

Many of us put off doing any estate planning. When we are young, many of us think we will live forever, and that estate planning is therefore irrelevant. When we are old, many of us just don't want to think about it. However, if you do no estate planning, you can leave your loved ones with an absolute mess. So, I would recommend that you consider some estate planning.

Estate planning can get very complicated and technical, particularly if you are planning to reduce estate taxes. It is easy to get caught up in all the jargon and technicalities and lose sight of what is the most important thing in estate planning. To my way of thinking, the most important thing in estate planning is not necessarily avoiding the estate tax or setting up the perfect trust, it is trying to maintain and improve the harmony and lives of your loved ones at the end of your life and after you are gone. That is what I think you should focus on in your estate planning.

The lives of your loved ones will also be easier if there is one place that your loved ones know to look for all of your estate planning documents and paperwork. So, try to put all of your estate planning documents and paperwork in one place, and be sure to let your loved ones know where that one place is. You may also want to consider if you want to leave the list of usernames and passwords so that your loved ones can access your online information.

ESTATE PLANNING DOCUMENTS

Typically, you have three legal estate planning documents, your financial power of attorney, your health care power of attorney, and your will.

Also, if you are part of an unmarried couple, you should know that unless you have these legal documents your loved one may have no legal rights or input over your finances or your healthcare, and may not get any of your property under most states' laws.

Financial Power of Attorney

When you are conscious and rational, you are in charge of your finances. But what about when you are not? A financial power of attorney is a legal document that gives someone else control over your finances. Typically, it is written so that someone else has control over your finances only if you cannot make your own decisions. You pretty much can have the financial power of attorney say exactly under what circumstances someone else has control of your finances.

Obviously, you want to choose an honest, trustworthy, and competent person who has the time and inclination to be your financial power of attorney holder. It is a good idea to choose at least one backup to your financial power of attorney holder in case your first choice is unable or unwilling to act for you if the time comes.

Healthcare Power of Attorney

Medical technology can keep us alive for longer and longer these days. This is generally, but not always, a good thing. When you are conscious and rational, you get to make your own health care decisions. But, what about when you are not? This is where a healthcare power of attorney which is also known as a medical power of attorney comes in. A healthcare power of attorney is a legal document that gives someone else control over your healthcare if you cannot communicate what you would like to have happen. It sometimes is combined with a financial power of attorney, but generally is a separate document.

Again, you can pretty much have the healthcare power of attorney say exactly under what circumstances you want it to apply. You want to have a trustworthy and competent person who has the time and inclination to be your healthcare power of attorney holder. You may also want to consider choosing someone who shares your values regarding healthcare and end of life decisions. It would be a good idea if you talked with your potential health care power of attorney holders and explained to them your value system and what they should consider in making your healthcare and end of life decisions. Again, it is a good idea to choose at least one backup in case your first choice is unable or unwilling to act for you if the time comes.

A healthcare power of attorney is not a living will. A living will is a document that deals with a very limited end of life situation. Living wills have occasionally been misinterpreted by healthcare providers as do not resuscitate orders. A healthcare power of attorney is much broader than a living will. Your healthcare can have many complicated and nuanced decisions that have to be made. I think that a health care power of attorney is far better than a living will. If you have a healthcare power of attorney and have communicated your wishes to your power holders, you do not need a living will.

Will

A will is a legal document that says who gets your property when you die if the property is not already transferred by some other legal mechanism. A will does not always control who gets all of the property that you own when you die. Some of your property may be transferred by beneficiary designation or the way it is legally titled regardless of what you say in your will.

For example, if you have made a beneficiary designation for your IRA or pension plan or life insurance policy, that beneficiary designation will override whatever you say in your will regardless of how recently you made your will or what your intentions are. Another example is if you own property with other people as joint tenants with right of survivorship. What joint tenants with right of survivorship legally means is that if one of the people who own the property dies, the part of the property that person used to own goes automatically to the remaining property owners.

So, when you make or update your will, you also want to look at all of your beneficiary designations and legal titling of your property and make sure that everything reflects your current thinking.

WHAT HAPPENS IF YOU HAVE NO WILL?

About half of us die without a will. So, what happens then? Each state has different rules, known as intestacy laws, that say who gets your property if you die without a will. Again, beneficiary designations and some legal titling such as joint tenants with right of survivorship generally override each state's intestacy laws. Really generally, most state's intestacy laws leave your property to some combination of your surviving spouse and children.

You are pretty much guaranteeing your loved ones more hassle if you die without a will. First, your loved ones will generally have to prove to some court that you had no will. Proving the nonexistence of anything can be very tricky from a logic point of view. Then, your loved ones will have to live with that court splitting your property according to whatever state's intestacy laws control your estate. This result may be very different from what you and they would have wanted. So, it is a good idea to have a will.

MAKING YOUR WILL

You can pretty much say anything you want in your will. Be sure to have lots of backups in your will. If you leave all of your property to one person, and that person dies before you, well, what then? If you want your trusted friend to be your personal representative to carry out your will and your trusted friend is unable or unwilling to do that, well, what then? Most people only update their will after many years. So, think long-term when you write your will, even if you intend to update your will in a year or two.

It is a good idea to periodically pull out your will and see how the property you currently own would be distributed under your will as it is written, and who would be in charge of various things under your will. Ideally, you change your will every time your life has a major change or you change what you would like to have happen under your will.

You can have your will written using software that costs less than $100, or you can spend thousands of dollars on a will drawn up by an estate attorney who is a fellow of the American College of Trust and Estate Counsel, or many alternatives between these two ends of the spectrum.

How do you choose how to write your will? First, how much money do you have to spend on writing a will and your other estate planning documents? If you only can spend a small amount, then the cheaper software solution is probably, but not always, better than nothing. On the other hand, if you want your will and other estate planning documents done really right and the peace of mind is worth the attorney's fees, find a competent and experienced estate attorney in the state you live in to write your will.

Second, what is the total value of your property? If the total value of your total property consists of a used phone and some beat up furniture, you probably do not need a top estate attorney. On the other hand, if the total value of your total property is so high that your estate is looking at paying state or federal estate taxes, you definitely need a competent and experienced estate attorney to help you. Finally, considering who you want to leave your property to, and who might feel they should have gotten more, what are the odds that someone will be unhappy enough with your will to challenge it in court? If you think your will is going to be challenged in court, then using a competent and experienced estate attorney to help write your will is a good idea.

If you decide to have your will done by software, the market leader for this type of software is Quicken Willmaker Plus. It is updated each year on more or less the same cycle as new cars. The current version of the software is the 2014 version. It is available to buy for less than $100.

If you decide to have your will done by an attorney, in my opinion, you should choose an attorney in the state you live in who has worked on estate planning full-time for a minimum of five years. Like choosing a tax professional, it is best that the estate attorney you choose has many other clients who are in your tax situation. If you are in a very complicated estate planning situation, you may wish to consider an attorney who is a fellow of the American College of Trust and Estate Counsel. Their website with a current web address of www.actec.org lists their fellows by state.

An experienced and competent estate attorney knows much about estate planning, but may know very little about what you are trying to accomplish with your estate planning. Be sure that your estate attorney has a good understanding of how you view the people you want to leave your property to, all the property you own or control, any property you may one day inherit, and exactly what you are trying to accomplish with your estate planning. Remember, the most important thing in the estate planning is trying to maintain and improve the harmony and lives of your loved ones at the end of your life and after you are gone.

PROBATE, INCOME TAXES AND ESTATE AND GIFT TAXES

Most of us tend to get the three related, but different, things in estate planning confused. These three things are probate, income taxes, and estate and gift taxes.

Probate

Probate is the legal process that determines who will own your property after you die if that property is not already transferred by something like a beneficiary designation or legal titling such as joint tenancy with right of survivorship. If you have a will, probate make sure that your will is followed. If you have no will, probate will apply your state's intestacy laws to distribute your property. During probate, any debts you owe at the time of your death are either generally paid or wiped out. Typically, probate records are public records, and anyone with enough persistence can normally see them. The hassle and cost of the probate process varies considerably by state.

If you want to avoid most of the probate process, one workaround is to create a living trust. Very generally, a living trust is a trust you create that you totally control, and that owns your property. A living trust can be used in states with a high hassle and high cost probate process to avoid most of the probate process. On the other hand, if you live in a state, like I do, with a pretty good probate process, you generally create a living trust only if you do not want your financial information to be public or you are concerned about someone contesting your will. Do not create or transfer any property to a living trust unless you have first consulted with an experienced and competent estate attorney in the state you live in.

Income Taxes

Generally, if you give a gift to anyone, or if your estate transfers your property to your heirs, there are no income taxes to pay. Generally, if you inherit anything, receive a gift, or collect on a life insurance policy, you have no income taxes to pay.

One exception to this is if you inherit something that is technically known as income in respect of a decedent or IRD income. Examples of the IRD income are traditional IRAs and pension plans, but not Roth IRAs or Roth pension plans. If you inherit a traditional IRA or pension plan, you do not have to pay income taxes when you first inherit the property. However, when you take money out of the inherited traditional IRA or pension plan, you do have to pay income taxes on what you take out.

Estate And Gift Taxes

Only about 2% of the estates in the United States pay estate taxes. But, for those estates that do have to pay the estate tax, the estate tax can really bite.

The estate tax is generally a tax that your estate owes on everything that you owned when you died, plus, potentially, life insurance policies on your life. Currently and generally, you only have to pay an estate tax to the federal government if the net fair market value of your property and potentially any payouts on life insurance policies on your life right before you die is greater than $5,250,000. Currently and generally, there is a federal estate tax of 40% on the amount above $5,250,000.

A long time ago, people figured out that an estate tax is only a tax on the property that you own when you die. So, if you give away all of your property before you die, you do not own any property when you die and therefore your estate does not owe any estate tax. This is all true. However, this is also why we also have the federal gift tax that works alongside the federal estate tax to keep you from doing this if you will owe federal estate tax.

The federal gift tax generally applies if your estate would have owed some federal estate tax, but you gave away part or all of your property before you died. Generally, you will only need to pay gift taxes if you make gifts of more than $5,250,000 during your life. So, the federal gift tax, like the federal estate tax, is not something that most of us need to worry about.

Now, the IRS has enough on its plate without tracking every gift everyone makes in this country during their life just in case the federal gift tax will apply. So, before any gift that you make even begins to get on the radar of the federal gift tax, the total gifts that you make to any one person in any calendar year have to exceed $14,000. In other words, each of us can give up to $14,000 to any person every year before there is anything that needs to be tracked or reported for the federal gift tax.

In addition to the federal estate tax, some states also have their own state estate tax. For example, in the state that I live in, there is a state estate tax if the net fair market value of your property and potentially any payouts on life insurance on your life right before you die is greater than $2 million. In my state, the state estate tax rate begins at 15% and goes up to 19% for amounts over $9 million.

So, if you lived in my state, and your estate was valued at more than $9 million, your estate would pay combined estate taxes at a 59% (40% +19%) tax rate on the part of your estate valued at more than $9 million. So, you can see why the estates that do have to worry about paying estate taxes really have to worry about it.

If you think your estate may owe estate taxes, you should get advice from and have your will prepared by an experienced and competent estate attorney who lives in your state. There are a variety of ways to reduce or even eliminate your estate's potential estate tax. Generally, if you do that, you will probably pay your estate attorney thousands of dollars in fees to further complicate your financial life, but you will also reduce your estate's potential estate tax.

LAST WORDS

Thank you for taking the time to read this book. I hope that you enjoyed it. More importantly, I hope you gained some lasting value by reading it. As I said before, I do not think the basic principles of financial security are all that complicated.

I am going off to do some other things with my life, and will no longer be here to answer questions and provide guidance. Hopefully, this book will give you some idea of what I would have said if I was here. I wish you the best of luck in the future in becoming financially secure and reaching your goals and dreams.

Made in the USA
Charleston, SC
05 October 2013